TRAUMA RECOVERY
WORKBOOK FOR TEENS

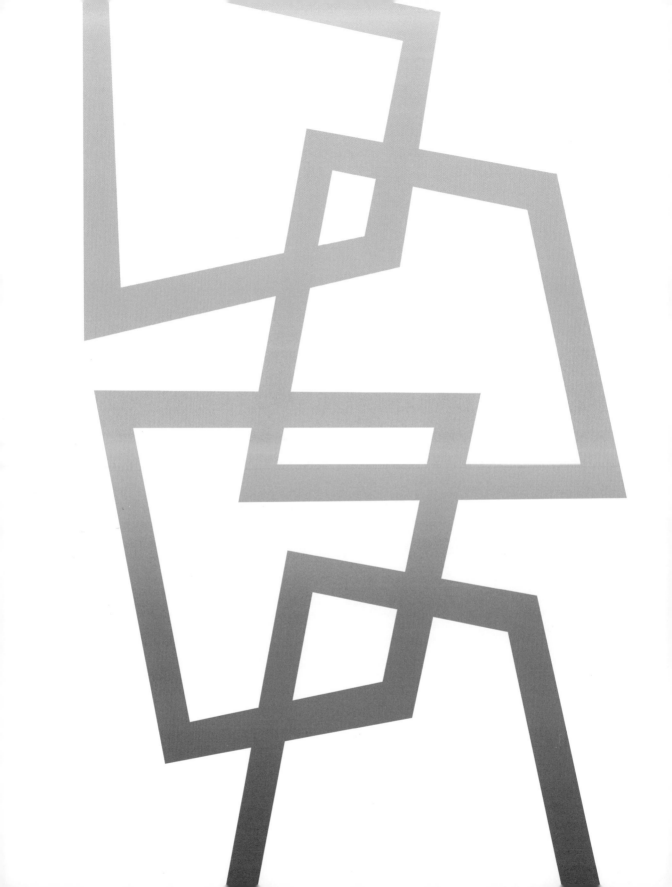

TRAUMA recovery WORKBOOK for TEENS

Exercises to Process Emotions, Manage Symptoms, and Promote Healing

DEBORAH VINALL, PsyD, LMFT

callisto
publishing
an imprint of Sourcebooks

Published by Callisto Publishing LLC C/O Sourcebooks LLC
P.O. Box 4410, Naperville, Illinois 60567-4410
(630) 961-3900
callistopublishing.com

Printed and bound in China
OGP 2

To Luke,
my favorite teenager in the world,
with all my love.

CONTENTS

INTRODUCTION

Dear Reader,

I'm so glad you've decided to move toward facing and healing from the trauma you've experienced—and so sorry you've faced such deep pain already in your life. I understand, both personally and professionally, how life changing trauma can be. I also know, both from my personal journey as well as from helping hundreds of others, that healing is possible. You won't always feel this way, and the pain you're experiencing won't always affect you as it does now.

   I began working with teens in my early twenties, because I knew how much I had needed a caring adult to help me in my own teenage years. I quickly realized that a sympathetic face was not enough to help the troubled teens I encountered, and I went back to school to earn a Bachelor of Arts in Human Development, a Master of Arts in Marriage, Family, and Child Therapy, and a Psychology Doctorate. Along the way, I worked with teens living in residential treatment facilities and foster care settings who had endured physical, sexual, and emotional abuses. I conducted award-winning research across the country on the impacts of surviving a mass shooting, including several prominent school shootings, and the best treatment approaches to help survivors heal. Now, in my outpatient private practice, I work with both adolescents and adults who have experienced many kinds of trauma, such as wildfires, mass shootings, dating violence, medical trauma, child abuse, animal attacks, and sexual assault.

I am sharing my experience so that you have an idea of whom you are "working with" as you go through this book. You should never trust someone simply because they tell you to, but perhaps this information will help you decide whether you feel that you can or are willing to trust me and this book.

It is important to keep in mind that this book is not a replacement for therapy. There are some layers of healing that can only happen through the interpersonal, face-to-face relationship that therapy provides. Nevertheless, this book will strengthen you with tools that can help you heal, make therapy more effective, and guide you in developing coping skills that will help you manage and diminish the impact of your symptoms.

In this book, you will learn more about what trauma is and how it affects you. You will find numerous resources, including concrete strategies you can begin to use right away. This book can also be a safe, private place to reflect on and work through some of your painful thoughts and feelings about what happened. Take your time as you work through this book. Check in with yourself often. If you become too flooded—experiencing such strong emotions and memories that you feel overwhelmed—give yourself permission to pause, take a break, and go do something that comforts you. There is always time for healing. Just take it one breath at a time.

HOW TO USE THIS BOOK

In this book, you'll find six chapters. Each chapter covers a different aspect of healing from trauma. You'll learn what trauma is and how it affects you. You'll tune into your emotions, thoughts, and actions. You'll find stories, drawn from real life (but not an exact retelling of any single person's story, to protect others' privacy), of teens who have experienced different traumas. Each chapter contains exercises to help you directly apply the concepts, affirmations to reflect on, and key take-aways to summarize the information in the chapter.

You'll probably get the most out of this book if you read it in order, so that you can build on what you've already learned and practiced. However, please feel free to return to earlier pages as often as needed. As healing begins, it's often necessary to rehearse certain ideas or revisit particular points that are challenging. This is not failure but a normal part of growth. Give yourself permission to listen to your instinct as it whispers what you need.

Again, this book cannot be a replacement for having a professional therapist partner to help you walk toward healing. I know that working through a book privately may feel safer right now than trusting someone new. And this is a great place to start! But do consider finding someone to join you on this path—whether now or later—and share with them what you are learning and developing through this workbook. There is no shame in seeking help—in fact, it shows great courage. We are all relational creatures—hurt most deeply in broken relationships but healing most fully through healthy relationships. You'll find some resources in the back to help in your search for a good therapist, and in chapter 2, you'll find some powerful therapy approaches that can help transform your life.

Check in with yourself often as you move through this workbook. Take deep breaths before, during, and after engaging with the exercises. Don't rush through—give yourself time. You can heal, one little step at a time. By picking up this book, you've already begun!

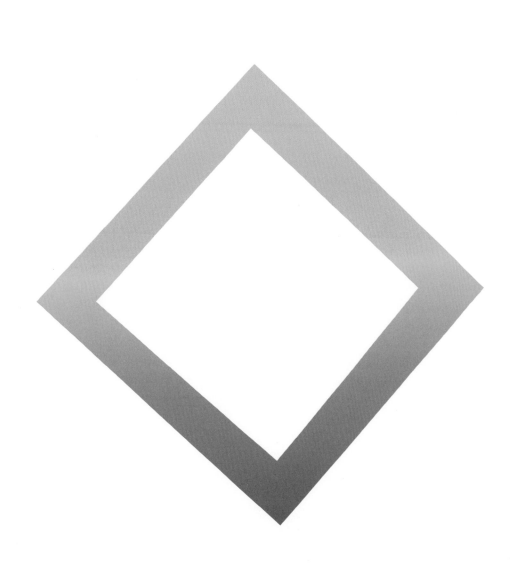

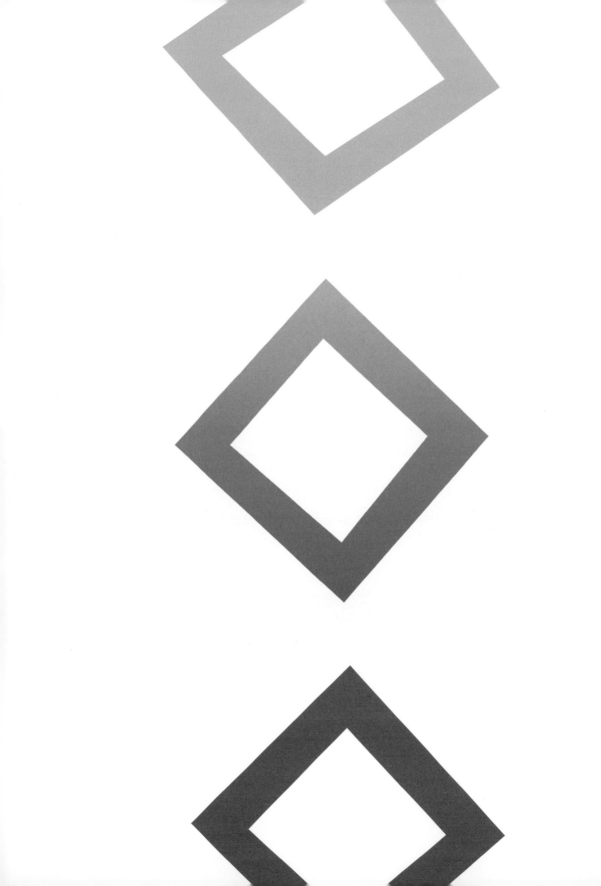

CHAPTER 1

THE TRUTH ABOUT TRAUMA

There are many sources of trauma and many ways that trauma may impact you. In this chapter, you'll learn what trauma is and explore the physical, cognitive, and emotional ways it affects you. As you engage with this chapter, I hope you will gain a greater understanding of and compassion for yourself—essential ingredients for healing.

What Is Trauma?

Trauma is anything that overwhelms your ability to cope with and integrate an experience at the time that it happens. When you experience a normal event, you file it away in your memory where you can recall it at will, without it being constantly on your mind. For example, if I ask you to think of your first day of school, an image probably springs to mind immediately, even though you were unlikely to have been thinking of it until now. However, when something is experienced as trauma, your usual memory-filing capability is fried, and you may continue to experience sensory fragments of the event for months or even years without intervention. Sensory fragments are memory experiences from any of your five senses—smells, tastes, physical sensations, sounds, or images that flash through your mind. These make an event that happened in the past feel like it *just* happened, is still happening, or is about to recur at any minute. Because the experience is not filed away like a normal memory, it continues to intrude on or interrupt your daily life in highly distressing ways.

Teen Trauma

As a teen, trauma impacts you in unique ways. Because you have less control over your life than an adult, you may be uniquely vulnerable to trauma. In fact, some studies, such as one by Sherry Hamby and associates, suggest that young people are the most traumatized group. You may or may not live with supportive family and have no control over who makes up this important inner support circle. If you are someone who lacks healthy, supportive connections at home, trauma will likely impact you more profoundly.

Another challenge as a teen who has faced trauma is that you may not have a wide repertoire of coping skills or ways to deal with the heightened emotions that trauma triggers. You have faced something terrible, something for which you were not yet ready (or for which perhaps no one would ever be). This is uniquely unsettling. Stay with me, and as you work through this book, you will develop some of those skills to help you cope.

In addition, your brain is still rapidly changing and developing. This means that traumatic experiences are imprinted in the brain in deeply formative ways, shaping who you are as you move toward adulthood. But take heart: addressing your trauma while still in adolescence can lead to profound healing due to this same mental flexibility. Thanks to this greater *neuroplasticity*, teens in therapy often see healing changes faster than adults! Choosing the courageous path of facing your experience and working on healing while you are still a teenager can free you from being held back by painful symptoms and empower you to become even stronger as you continue to grow.

When a bone breaks, it will heal. If it is not set in alignment before it heals, you will experience impairment for life. If it is properly aligned and then heals, the point where the bone broke will be stronger than ever before. Healing from psychological trauma works the same way.

You *can* heal, and you can develop resilience, skills, and strength that will stay with you for life. The exercises in this book, along with professional therapy, are the "alignment" that can prevent you from suffering debilitating effects. You've got this. In your weakness, you will find strength.

RENÉ'S STORY

René was fourteen when a wildfire ripped through his mountain community, destroying every home in its path. The image of angry flames pursuing and consuming as he and his mom fled was seared into his memory.

Tossing and turning on the cot in his cousin's bedroom, he couldn't shut out the images or the feelings of terror. He stared up at the smoke detector in the ceiling, watching for its intermittent red blink to assure him it was active. Sometimes he felt sure he smelled smoke and quietly prowled about checking for fire. Sunlight dawned before he was finally able to sleep. He awoke the next day exhausted, irritable, and on edge.

At school, René couldn't concentrate. He was often angry, and his reputation changed from honor student to disciplinary problem. Friends backed away from his short temper, and René retreated into solitude, certain no one could understand anyway. Desperate to help, his mom made an appointment with a therapist to address the trauma underlying René's problems. Though nervous, René felt a tiny ray of hope peek through the storm clouds of his mind.

Trauma: Fact versus Fiction

To get a handle on what trauma *is*, it is also important to recognize what it is *not*. Contrary to what some may say, trauma is *not* weakness. Trauma is not something that just happens to veterans of war. You don't have to be shot at to become traumatized (although that certainly would cause trauma for most people). Trauma isn't something you can or should "just suck up and get over," nor is it something that will heal simply by thinking positively. Time does not "heal all wounds," but reprocessing traumatic memories and senses can.

Trauma is not "all in your head." Trauma is stored in the body throughout the nervous system. It can affect every cell of your body. Because of this, as you move through this workbook, pay attention not only to your thoughts, emotions, and memories but to your physical feelings as well.

Trauma can happen to anyone. Trauma is the natural result of any experience that poses a real or perceived threat to your life, safety, or sense of self. This causes changes in the brain—particularly in the *limbic* (emotional/motivational) system and the *hippocampus* (memory storage)—and is therefore as physical as it is emotional and mental. Trauma is real. By facing the truth, you give the trauma you experienced the serious attention it deserves so that you can heal and be free.

Types of Trauma

Trauma can result from many experiences. Anything that severely shakes your sense of safety may cause psychological trauma. You may suffer from chronic or acute post-traumatic stress, depending on what happened and when. *Developmental traumas* are experiences that begin in childhood and continue over a period of time, such as physical, sexual, or psychological abuse, whether from adults or peers. *Single-incident traumas* may result from accidents or assaults. *Existential trauma* occurs when a disaster threatens your life in indirect, yet serious ways. *Vicarious trauma* develops when you are directly exposed to a threat to the life or safety of someone else.

You may have experienced a single form of trauma or have compounded trauma from layered experiences. In fact, early developmental trauma may make you more vulnerable to experiencing later traumas and increase your susceptibility to developing post-traumatic stress disorder (PTSD) from subsequent incidents. Whatever the specifics of your experience, your trauma and your feelings are valid. You can heal, and you deserve to heal.

PHYSICAL ABUSE OR ASSAULT

Physical violence directly attacks your safety. If you have experienced physical violence, whether in an isolated incident or as part of an ongoing cycle of abuse, your overall sense of safety in the world is damaged. You may become jumpy and fearful of others, with a heightened sense of a need to protect yourself. It could become difficult to feel safe with others. The physical harm you have suffered may heal quickly while the psychological effects linger.

SEXUAL ABUSE OR ASSAULT

Sexual assault damages the lighthearted sense of safety you may have once enjoyed. Sexual assault or abuse attacks your sense of sovereignty, or ownership, over your body. This may cause you to feel as though there is nowhere safe to retreat to. When your body has been violated and even your own sensations feel unsafe, you may develop dissociative or out-of-body reactions to avoid and cope with the intensity of the physical memories. Additionally, sexual assault and abuse damages your ability to trust in relationships.

An important note: Sexual assault or rape is not only something that happens at the hands of a stranger. In fact, the vast majority of sexual assaults are perpetrated by someone well-known to you, such as a family member, church member, or date. Having had affectionate feelings toward the person who assaulted you does *not* mean that you wanted it to happen or that it was your fault. If you did not enthusiastically consent both in your heart and with words or actions, or if you initially were interested but changed your mind as things progressed, you experienced a sexual assault. This was *not* your fault.

CHILDHOOD ABUSE OR NEGLECT

Childhood abuse may take many forms. Abuse may show up as physical and sexual abuse, emotional or psychological abuse, or neglect. Abuse happens when someone with more power or authority uses their position to harm you. It may involve physical punishment or other violence. It could involve inviting you to watch sexual videos with them or to show or look at each other's naked bodies, sexual touch, or rape. Psychological, emotional, or verbal abuse takes the forms of constant criticism, verbal attacks, put-downs, name-calling, cursing at you, and insults. These abuses may be covered up with gaslighting, another form of psychological abuse, wherein the abuser denies what they have done and suggests that you are "crazy," too emotional, or overreacting. Finally, neglect occurs when your parent or caregiver fails to provide adequate and appropriate care in the forms of food, attention, supervision, or access to education or medical care.

If you have been growing up with one or more forms of abuse, please know that this is not okay! You are worth so much more than what has been shown to you. If you are still living in a home environment where these things are happening, please tell a trusted adult, such as a teacher at school, a doctor, or a counselor or therapist. You can also find a crisis hotline to call or text by turning to the resources section at the back of this book (page 164).

ACCIDENTS OR HEALTH CRISES

Perhaps you have experienced a serious accident or health crisis, either affecting your own body or someone very close to you and on whom you depend. The physical damage to your body may heal, leave scars, alter your lifestyle in a permanent way, or leave you fearful of recurrence. Such crises are overwhelming and may lead to trauma symptoms such as flashbacks or nightmares, which are indicators of an unresolved trauma that has exceeded your usual coping capacity.

DISASTERS OR POLITICAL UPHEAVAL

Trauma may also result from events happening not directly *to* you but around you. These events and disasters can make the world itself feel unsafe. Hurricanes, tornadoes, earthquakes, floods, epidemics and pandemics, political revolutions and uprisings, and war are all sources of existential trauma.

Depending on your exposure and the number of losses, other stressors, and supportive people in your life, the impact of the COVID pandemic and surrounding political unrest may have contributed to a broad sense of existential trauma as the usual fabric of society and daily life unraveled in 2020 and beyond. These changes upset the predictability of life and disconnected most teens from coping outlets and support systems, making any pre- or coexisting traumas worse.

COMMUNITY OR HOME VIOLENCE

Similar to the effects of disasters, violence in your community or in your home, even when not directed at you, can lead to psychological trauma. It is difficult to ever feel fully at ease, settled, or safe when violence is right at your door. If there is violence between the adults in your home, or within your neighborhood, your nervous system is likely to stay in a hyper-activated state, leaving you tense and on edge. Constant fearfulness for your own safety or the safety of a loved one is innately traumatizing, accentuated by the concrete traumas of hearing or seeing violent attacks. Because your brain has "mirror neurons" that allow you to sense what others are feeling, the mere observation of violence imprints vicarious trauma in your psyche.

JAMAL'S STORY

Jamal would never forget the moment he came in the door after school to find his dad unconscious. He had frantically called his mom, then 911, and started CPR while he waited for what seemed like endless minutes for the paramedics.

His dad never woke up, and the sense of helplessness and utter loneliness had never gone away. Jamal felt angry at his dad, yet blamed himself for not doing enough to save him. He kept having dreams of his father asking for help but being unable to reach him. Jamal dreaded coming home after school, unable to shake the sense of foreboding and flashback images linked to walking through that door. Sometimes, he'd see his mom asleep, and his heart would pound, his body would break into a cold sweat, and he felt like he would hyperventilate.

Jamal felt like a different person since his father's death, and he didn't like it. He didn't understand why he was so tense, angry, and on edge when his mother was sad, crying, and without energy. Why was his response so different?

The answer came to him in school, via a video played in his intro to psych class. Jamal's mind had been wandering, but when the speaker described PTSD, his head snapped up. A voice inside insisted, "That's me!" It helped a lot to realize he wasn't "crazy" or bad. His responses made sense.

How Trauma Affects You

Trauma affects each person differently. Your temperament, prior life experiences, age at which the trauma occurred, relationship to the person responsible, support systems, and resulting losses, as well as the type, severity, and duration of the trauma will all play a role in how it impacts you. For this reason, it is critical to lay aside comparisons and *should*s. There is no right or wrong way to react when something devastating happens to you, and no metric to determine whether an event should have caused trauma symptoms. With self-compassion, acknowledge how you feel and how the trauma impacts you. In facing these truths, with kindness to yourself, you can begin to heal.

As you read over the following descriptions of potential impacts on your body, mind, emotions, relationships, and spirituality, slow down and reflect on your personal reality. What resonates, and what does not? You may recognize some of the symptoms in yourself while others might not apply. You may experience many at the same time or have periods where none apply. As you read the descriptions, notice how the categories overlap and interact, with feelings impacting thoughts and physical changes connecting to feelings. Be honest as you inventory the effects in your life, so that you know where to begin as you take steps to overcome.

PHYSICAL

Trauma is stored in the body. Even if you try to push away the memories of what happened and deny or drown your feelings in drugs, alcohol, busyness, or overachievement, your body remembers. Your body will tell the story that you may not want to face.

The nervous system, which includes your brain and connects with the nerves in your muscles, skin, heart, and lungs, is central in response to trauma, both in the immediate moment and in the aftermath. It controls the rate of your breath and heart, preparing you to *fight* or *flee* from danger, or to slow everything down into a *freeze* response that facilitates hiding. These physiological reactions that helped you survive can become ingrained patterns in your body in response to false alarms of danger or perceived threat. Constantly being tensed in self-protection is exhausting while a triggered freeze reaction can induce a terrible sense of helplessness.

After exposure to trauma, a part of the brain called the *HPA* becomes hypersensitive, causing it to release more of the stress hormone *cortisol*. When traumatic stress goes untreated, this brain-hormone response continues to be activated, and the excess cortisol can lead to psychological symptoms such as depression and anxiety as well as physical conditions such as heart disease and autoimmune disorders. It also wears down your immune system, which can cause you to get sick more often.

Being constantly on alert and tense causes direct and immediate impacts on your body, too. You may notice headaches, sore muscles, and tightness in your jaw, neck, and shoulders. Some people develop patterns of *bruxism*, or teeth grinding, while asleep, which can wear down your teeth. You may experience stomachaches and changes to your digestion, such as nausea, diarrhea, or constipation.

Trauma will not allow you to simply hold it in and forget. Your body will express the truth and raise the alarm that something must change. Healing is needed.

EMOTIONAL

Trauma causes your nervous system to become dysregulated, meaning your natural processes of becoming excited or calming down after agitation can break down. Usually, your nervous system is like a dimmer light, fluctuating between bright, dark, and various levels of luminosity in between. When trauma happens, your emotions may become stuck at one extreme or the other—either with the light off, in a depressed state with too little energy, or with the light stuck at glaring brightness in an anxious state with excess energy.

When trauma results in PTSD, you may experience frequent or constant irritability, nervousness, jumpiness, anxiety, and a sense of being constantly on alert and unable to relax, always waiting for the next danger to come. You may have feelings of hopelessness, as if you have no future, and experience frequent crying spells.

MENTAL

The emotions you're feeling can make it difficult to concentrate. You may notice gaps in your memory, both surrounding the trauma itself, and of later events, making it hard to learn. School may become difficult if your mind is frequently elsewhere. Many trauma survivors experience flashbacks and intrusive memories—moments when images or other sensory pieces of the trauma such as smells or sounds suddenly invade the mind. Not only can this be highly distressing and emotionally painful, but it can also be disruptive to learning and focus.

In addition, you may find it difficult to relax enough to sleep well. When you do sleep, you may have nightmares that replay aspects of your experience or represent the feelings of terror through imaginary scenarios. Nightmares are different from dreams in that you typically awake without the dream resolving, flooded by terrified or disgusted feelings. Normally, dreams help you resolve ordinary stresses from your day through creative metaphorical imagery, but when trauma happens, nightmares result, with your mind too overwhelmed to find positive and helpful resolutions to the extraordinary stress.

SOCIAL

The effects of trauma ripple out into our social spheres. If you have been hurt by someone else, you may find it difficult to trust others. Mood changes, such as increased irritability, may push others away. Many people who have experienced trauma worry that others won't understand. They are afraid to burden others with their intense feelings or to cause them worry. Sometimes those who have gone through a collective trauma, such as a school shooting, worry about talking with those who went through it with them for fear of triggering their friends and causing them to feel worse. For all these reasons, it can be tempting to withdraw, or *fade*, from others at a time when you need social support more than ever.

People who experience interpersonal trauma may develop a *fawn* response, where you learn to be submissive and try to please others to avoid anger. Some may engage with others in what psychologist Connie Johnshoy-Currie identifies as *flocking behavior*, or taking on a caretaking role and sublimating their own need for emotional healing by playing counselor to others. Still more survivors go the opposite direction and take a defensive or offensive posture and engage in *fighting* to avoid being a victim ever again.

Do you see yourself in any of these postures? Do you fade, fawn, flock, or fight? As you draw connections from your social struggles to your trauma response, you become empowered to begin to make changes and build satisfying relationships. You will explore ways to strengthen your social connections in greater depth in chapter 5.

SPIRITUAL

When you go through an earth-shattering experience, it can shake your foundational beliefs about life, the world, and your faith. Some religious people question their beliefs while others rely even more strongly on their faith and draw comfort from it. Shifts in your sense of meaning in the world can be painful, yet they can also be signs of post-traumatic growth as you examine and deepen your understanding of meaning in life. If this is part of your adjustment, know that you are not alone.

Checklist: Trauma Symptoms

Perhaps you are still questioning whether what you went through and how you are feeling counts as trauma. To help you better understand your experience, I've created this checklist. This is not an official diagnostic assessment, but a self-reflection tool to help you consider your experiences.

	NEVER	SOMETIMES	OFTEN
I have felt like I was in danger.			
I have seen something awful happen to someone else.			
Flashbacks or unwanted memories come into my mind out of nowhere.			
I have nightmares.			
I am jumpy and easily startled.			
I am more watchful and alert than most people.			
It's hard to trust others.			
It's hard to concentrate.			
I feel irritable.			
I feel like I'm a bad person.			
I avoid things and places that remind me of certain memories.			
I don't like to talk about the past.			
I feel disconnected from others, including my friends and family.			
I have a sense that perhaps I won't live a long time.			
I feel like I'm not real.			
I feel disconnected from my body and the world around me.			
I feel like I'm watching myself from outside or above, like a dream.			

If you have a lot of answers in the "sometimes" or "often" categories, you've probably been significantly affected by a terrible experience or pattern of events. A few answers in the "sometimes" or "often" category could point to different things besides trauma, but if they stand together with many of the other symptoms listed, it's probably linked to what you went through.

If you answered "often" to all of the last three questions, I strongly urge you to work through this book with the support of a licensed therapist. While these experiences are common reactions to trauma, if you feel this way most of the time, focusing on your trauma without support could make those feelings worse, and make it difficult to get the most out of this book. A therapist who specializes in trauma will be able to help you face the past without shutting down or becoming too flooded to continue. No matter what you went through, you *can* and are worthy to heal.

I Have a Question . . .

It's been two years since I was raped. I am dating someone new, and they are really great. I thought by now I'd be over it, but I can't get the memories out of my mind. Sometimes when I'm touched, I feel like I'm being assaulted all over again even though I know the person I'm dating now would never do that. Will I always feel this way? Am I permanently damaged?

This is such a painful, invasive, and terrifying thing to experience. What you're describing are normal reactions to an abnormal experience. Trauma effects can linger for some time. If they don't go away after a month, you might be diagnosed with PTSD.

PTSD doesn't fade with time alone. It highlights that what you experienced was truly severe and has impacted you, *but* it does not have to be a life sentence. One of the reasons I love doing trauma therapy is that when the source of the problem is known, it can be healed! Trauma symptoms are remarkably responsive to the right therapy. You *can* heal, put away distressing memories, find a sense of safety in your body, and enjoy intimate embrace once again. Don't give up. You are *not* damaged goods. You are worthy of comfort and healing.

It's okay to not feel okay.

I can heal.

I will overcome.

Key Takeaways

- Trauma is any experience that overwhelms your ability to cope in healthy ways.

- Trauma shows up in changes to how the memory is stored.

- Trauma can happen to anyone—it is not about character, strength, or weakness.

- Trauma impacts adolescents uniquely due to the vulnerability of being in positions of dependency and the ongoing brain development happening at the same time.

- Trauma may result from child abuse, physical or sexual assault, natural or man-made disasters, home or community violence, medical or health crises, accidents, and more.

- Trauma impacts your thoughts, feelings, body, relationships, and spirituality.

- Trauma may change you, but it does not condemn you to suffer forever—you can heal!

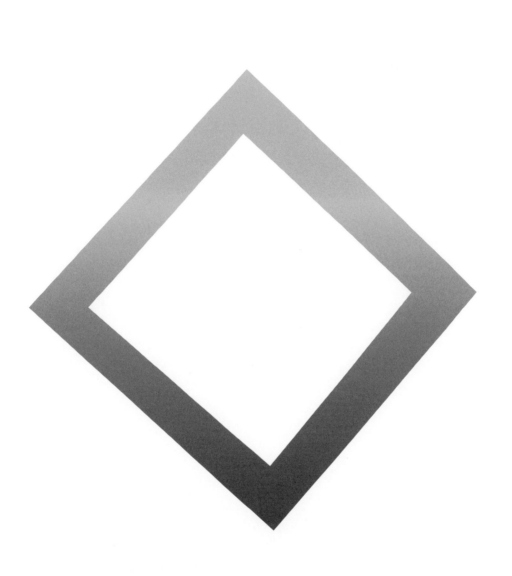

CHAPTER 2

ADDRESSING YOUR TRAUMA

In this chapter, I'll present a more in-depth look at the emotional impacts of trauma. You will learn how to face, connect with, and work through some of your intense feelings and find ways to cope when you're overwhelmed. Finding the strength and inner resources to allow yourself to feel and move through your emotions as you face the painful memories is key to healing. Things may be hard right now, but don't give up!

It's Not Your Fault

What you went through was undeniably terrible. To make matters worse, you may struggle with the sense that you were somehow at fault or should have done more in the face of it. Such thoughts make the feelings connected to the memory more painful. I have worked with people who survived mass shootings, emotional abuse, kidnapping, ferocious dog attacks, assaults, and trafficking, and no matter how different the trauma, this theme consistently emerges.

And it is *false*. What happened was *not* your fault. Whether you were the victim of a predatory person or a natural disaster, you are not to blame.

ADDRESSING GUILT AND SHAME

When the world feels out-of-control and you feel unsafe, it is natural to try to regain a sense of control by imagining you have powers you do not have. It's not a conscious decision, but you resist helpless feelings by telling yourself that you should have known, that you could have done more to resist the situation or save others, or that you somehow brought it upon yourself.

This is an illusion—a false sense of control—that comes at a steep cost. Self-blame carries with it intense feelings of guilt and shame. Guilt says it is somehow your fault, and shame goes a step further and persuades you that because of this event, you are a bad person. Such beliefs are a crushing weight.

No matter what you did or did not do, others abusing or attacking you is *never* your fault. You did not invite that. You do not carry responsibility for the choices or behaviors of others. Likewise, when disaster strikes, your sole job is to survive. And you've done that! No other responsibilities or expectations were on you.

Sometimes trauma results from an accident or incident that occurred while you were doing something you know you could get into trouble for doing, such as sneaking out after curfew, driving without a license, or using substances such as alcohol. This can make the issue of self-blame trickier to sort out. What is crucial to hold on to is that even with such regrets, you did not *intend* to cause harm to others, such as in a car crash, nor did you consent to assault. You are only responsible for the actions you took, but *not* for what happened next. Give yourself grace to let that go.

HEALING STRATEGIES

Often, it can be difficult to connect what your mind knows with what your heart feels. For example, many rape survivors *know* it was their attacker's fault but *feel* guilty. Trauma causes fragmentation in how our minds process information about the experience, and so thoughts (in the *prefrontal cortex* at the front of the brain) fail to communicate effectively with feelings (in the deep core regions of the brain's *limbic system*).

If this is your experience, you might benefit from powerful brain-based therapies that stimulate the creative and analytical sides of the brain at the same time while creating a sense of soothing. Rather than simply talking about what happened, these therapies help you focus quietly on multiple aspects of the trauma, such as thoughts, feelings, physical sensations, images, sounds, and smells, that are held in different brain regions. When you activate all these resources of your mind at once, what your logical brain knows is communicated deeply with your feeling brain, and guilt or shame is released in a profound, lasting way.

Brainspotting is a form of therapy that uses targeted points in your visual field to help you access unprocessed trauma memories. It typically employs *bilateral*, or side to side, sound stimulation using headphones through which soothing music travels from one ear to the other and back while you mindfully tune into your feelings and bodily memory.

Eye Movement Desensitization and Reprocessing (EMDR) also uses bilateral stimulation, typically through eye movements, taps, or tones, to help you access and process trauma at a deeply felt level while making new associations, examining harmful beliefs, and developing new insights that help alleviate emotional distress.

JADE'S STORY

When school reopened after the mass shooting, Jade avoided her classmates. She stuck to herself at lunch and avoided making eye contact. The words, "It's all my fault," kept drumming in her head.

In therapy, she explained how she had been friends with the shooter in middle school, but they'd drifted apart when they moved to the larger high school. "I should have known," Jade whispered, staring at her hands. "If I'd stayed friends with him, maybe I could have stopped him—or at least warned everyone."

"Hmm," the therapist reflected. "What do you feel right now as you think of that?"

"Guilty," Jade mumbled.

"And where do you feel those guilty feelings in your body?"

Jade considered the unusual question, then placed a hand on her belly. "Right here. It feels like a rock."

"Just notice that feeling, and see what else comes up," the therapist responded, as she guided Jade to let her eyes rest on a fixed spot where the feelings were strongest. Jade listened to the soothing music fade from one headphone to the other and back as her mind floated back over her relationship with the classmate and the events of that horrible day.

As Jade allowed herself to feel her feelings and listen to her body, the knot in her stomach loosened. She began to think of his responsibility. Anger replaced guilt, rising in strength and then subsiding too. As she shared these thoughts, feelings, and senses with her therapist, allowing the tears to fall in grief over her lost classmates, a feeling of peace gradually emerged. "I did the best I could to be a friend," Jade concluded. "He made his own choices."

I Have a Question . . .

I left the gate unlocked and my dog got out and was hit by a speeding car. How can I ever forgive myself for what I did to him?

The question of forgiveness is so important. But let's back up first. The words "what I did to him" take an awful lot of responsibility for something that clearly wasn't intentional. You obviously love your dog very much and never wanted any harm to come to him. It sounds like you made a mistake—certainly one with steep consequences—but definitely not a malicious choice.

You also mention a speeding car, though all the blame is directed at yourself. Can you accept that your oversight with the gate was only one piece of the chain of events? Having a realistic assessment of the situation is an important starting place.

It's so good that you want to forgive yourself because it suggests space for self-compassion, and self-compassion is essential for healing. Imagine that the gate was left open by someone else whom you dearly love. Now take the empathy you might feel for that person and allow yourself to receive it.

Fill in the Blanks: Let's Talk about Self-Love

Misplaced guilt, shame, and self-blame are debilitating outcomes of experiencing trauma. They do not coexist well with self-love. And you are worthy of love! Right now, without condition. Not "almost" or "sort-of" or "soon." Just the way you are: perfectly imperfect.

Self-love is the root of self-compassion, which is the antidote to shame. To help nurture your self-love, let's spend a little time in creative connection with your inner self.

Dear _____, I'm sorry I've been so hard on you lately.
(your name here)

I want you to know that you are special and important. One thing I appreciate

about you is _____. You're so good

at _____ and _____.

And do you know what others say about you? Your friends like how you

are _____

and _____.

You truly make the world a better place by _____

_____. I'm proud of you for _____

_____.

I want you to know that I'm going to work on being kinder to you. One way I'll

do this is by _____.

When you feel sad, I'll _____

to comfort you. It's okay if you cry. I'm not ashamed of your tears.

I also need to tell you I forgive you for _____

_____. I understand why it hap-

pened. I don't blame you anymore.

Thank you for _____.

I'm so glad you _____.

With love,

_____

How did it feel to work through that letter? Perhaps it wasn't easy. You might not be sure what to put in some blanks (although I encourage you to try!). Some ideas might not feel quite true yet. That's okay. Spend a little time with it now, and then come back to it later and add to it. Read it over with compassion and sincerity, maybe even out loud. Look at yourself in a mirror and remind yourself "I am a person of great value," quieting any self-critical thoughts.

Practice: Releasing My Guilt

When you feel guilt associated with a trauma you endured, you may be over-inflating a small aspect of personal responsibility. For example, if someone was kidnapped when they stayed out after curfew, most would not argue that it is their fault they were forced into a stranger's vehicle.

Use the circle to create a pie chart, marking off sections that feel realistic in proportion to the responsibility of the various people involved in your trauma. Use as many sections as are appropriate to your situation—some scenarios are more complicated than others.

What did you notice as you did this activity? Did anything surprise you? Can you let yourself off the hook a little bit and accept that it was not all your fault? Will you offer yourself forgiveness for any mistakes you made?

Understanding Your Emotions

The terrible thing or things you went through and all that it cost will naturally bring up many strong feelings. You might experience extremes of emotions, swinging from sadness and grief to anger or fear. This is completely natural and totally okay. Sometimes you might feel no negative emotions and feel happy despite it all. That's okay, too. As you progress through the book, there will be space to explore these feelings, to better understand yourself, and to find ways to accept, soothe, and cope with all that you feel. It is okay to not always feel okay. Know that you will not always feel this way.

WHAT AM I FEELING?

Trauma can leave you raw. You may find yourself constantly angry, irritable, and on edge. Perhaps you find yourself prone to episodes of unquenchable crying. You may feel jumpy and anxious, with a pounding or fluttery heart, shaky hands, and shallow breathing. You may be *hypervigilant*, or always on alert, looking for signs of danger in a subconscious behavioral pattern that makes it impossible to ever fully relax. After a significant trauma, many things feel more threatening than they might otherwise. The fundamental feeling that stays with you after trauma is a sense of being unsafe.

You may feel fine one moment and then be triggered by some cue to the traumatic event that sends you into fight, flight, or freeze mode. This can show up in your life as yelling or getting into fights, an urge or action of running away, wanting to escape or go home, or a sense of helplessness when you feel like you simply can't find the words to say anything or find the strength to move to get out of an uncomfortable situation. Following such incidents, you might find yourself inexplicably crying, as your body and brain seek release of all those stress hormones and tension and flush it out with tears. Don't be ashamed of your tears—allowing yourself this natural release can be an act of self-care.

It is important to build your awareness of what you're feeling because what you recognize you gain a measure of control over. As you begin to understand and develop compassion for yourself, you begin to build the power of the *pause*. This is a critical space in which you might recognize the automatic feeling and be able to consider your needs in the moment and your options to caringly meet those needs.

The powerful feelings you are experiencing are remnants from the trauma, leftover pieces that are intense because of what has not yet been processed. These unresolved feelings can make the trauma feel immediate and ever present. When your nervous system signals that you are still in danger, even though you cognitively know you are not, you will experience intense feelings as though you are. This is why it is so important to face the trauma so that it can be processed or moved from its frozen state into long-term memory.

HEALING STRATEGIES

To begin to shift feelings of being constantly in danger or of needing to stay hypervigilant to ward off danger, you must go back to the source. There are two ways of doing this, sometimes referred to as *top-down* and *bottom-up* approaches.

- **Bottom-up** means starting with the body by creating physical calm so that the nervous system learns to relax, which in turn tells the brain that the danger has passed, soothing the mind and emotions. Examples of bottom-up approaches that are proven to relax the nervous system and decrease stress include meditation, guided imagery, breathing techniques, and gentle movement such as stretching or yoga. Therapies such as Somatic Experiencing and Brainspotting are powerful bottom-up approaches that incorporate mindful bodily awareness with release of trauma memories.

- **Top-down** refers to starting in the brain by addressing the memories, so that the body and emotions shift in response. Talking or writing about the trauma while allowing yourself to remember and feel your feelings are top-down approaches. Trauma-Focused Cognitive Behavioral Therapy (TF-CBT) is considered the most effective pure top-down approach. Even more powerful are hybrid therapies, such as EMDR, which help you connect with your thoughts, memories, feelings, and gut sense of the experience all at once within the safety of a caring therapeutic relationship.

The first step in healing painful emotions is getting in touch with what you are feeling so that you can express and release it in healthy ways. Take your time with the following exercises, which will guide you in compassionately exploring your inner landscape.

Chart: My Emotions

Broadening your emotional vocabulary can help you identify and understand your emotions. Consider the emotions represented in the flower that follows. Each petal contains gradients of a core emotion, intensifying as you move outward. Which of these emotions have you experienced this week? Notice how distressing or pleasant each has felt.

MEDITATION PRACTICE

This first meditation exercise is designed simply to help you get in touch with your feelings. There is no right or wrong; no pass or fail. Simply be compassionate with yourself and notice what you are feeling with loving-kindness.

- Find a place to sit or lie down where you feel supported. Notice the texture and warmth, firmness or softness, of the surface on which you are sitting. Notice how your body connects to it—where you end and it begins. Bring your attention to every nerve, every cell that is making contact. Notice the feel of your clothing against your skin. Is it soft? Rough? Tight? Loose? Comfortable? Make any adjustments that will bring you greater ease.

- Bring your attention to your ears. What do you hear? Close your eyes for a moment to really tune into your hearing sense. What sounds are coming from inside? What do you hear outside? Are they sounds of nature or industry? Quiet? Loud? Distant or nearby?

- Take a deep breath in, feeling the warmth of the air drawing in through your nose. What is the smell of this place? Is it a comforting, familiar smell? Do scents drift in from other rooms? You might light a candle, spray perfume, or slice a piece of fruit to focus your sense of smell. Notice the emotions this brings you.

- Shift your attention once again to your internal bodily sensations. This time, notice what is happening inside. Perhaps place a hand on your heart and another on your stomach, noticing the rhythm of your heartbeat, the rise and fall of your chest. Is your breathing quick? Shallow? Deep? Do you hold your breath? Without forcing any changes, just notice it.

- Scan your body for any tension or tightness. Notice those feelings, and just sit with them. Without judgment, allow yourself to observe any emotions that connect with what your body is feeling. Pay attention to these signals with gentle awareness, noticing your connection to the world and to yourself.

Practice this regularly to ground yourself and increase your sense of con-nection to your body and emotions. This will build your self-awareness, decreasing reactivity and increasing your ability to find helpful ways to cope.

You can note any observations from your experience with this exercise in the lines below.

_____

_____

_____

_____

_____

_____

_____

_____

_____

_____

_____

Table: How and When I Feel

Use this log to record your emotions and increase your self-awareness of the connections between your experiences, thoughts, and feelings. You can make copies of it for your personal use before filling it in the first time, or copy the categories in a blank notebook.

WHAT HAPPENED	WHAT I THOUGHT	HOW I FELT	HOW INTENSE (1 TO 10)	HOW I REACTED

Breath Work: Square Breathing

There are many different breathing strategies that can help bring you a sense of calm. One simple technique is *square breathing*.

Use your finger to slowly trace along the edges of the square below, starting at the top left corner. As you move from left to right, slowly inhale through your nose. As your finger drops down the right side, hold the air in your lungs. Trace your finger across the bottom toward the left as you exhale slowly, and hold your lungs empty as you return to the starting point. Repeat this pattern five to ten times, noticing the change in your body, heart, and mind.

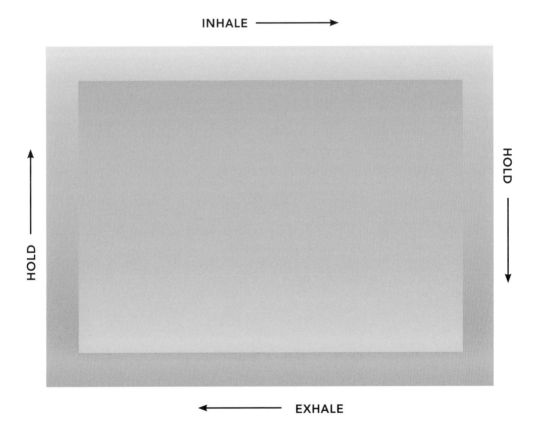

INHALE ⟶

HOLD

HOLD

⟵ EXHALE

Managing Your Stress and Anxiety

When you've faced a terrifying situation, you may become hyperalert to signs of danger around you. Things that might once have seemed nonthreatening become sources of anxiety. You may worry more, with an expanded awareness of all that could go wrong. These possibilities seem bigger than before, out of proportion with the actual risk of them happening. You might even be aware of that, but it truly feels like the worst might happen.

In addition, with intrusive memories taking up so much mental energy and making it difficult to concentrate, you might have new or increased struggles with school. Conflict with parents, caregivers, or teachers about grades and performance, or what might appear to them like not paying attention or not caring, can create a third layer of stress and compound your anxiety. Likewise, changes in your mood or fears that they won't understand might be causing problems with your friends. These secondary factors may create added sources of stress after trauma.

With so many potential sources of stress and anxiety, finding ways to cope is critical.

STRESSFUL IMPACTS

All this stress takes a toll on you. Your nervous system keeps your body tensed to respond to danger in self-protection, and you may experience digestive issues, stomachaches, tension headaches, sore muscles, dry mouth, faster heartbeat, and shallow breath. You might find it hard to relax and feel comfortable. Remaining hyperalert feels essential, yet it is exhausting, harming your mental and physical health.

While these symptoms are uncomfortable in the present, they can lead to even more serious effects over time. The constant flood of stress hormones will eventually leave you depleted, either causing a collapse from tension into depression or continuing in a constant state of anxiety. Continual exposure to stress hormones can lead to autoimmune disorders, hormone disruption (which can cause reproductive problems), heart disease, even heightened risk of cancer. You've been through enough; you certainly don't need all that.

But this doesn't have to be a prophecy of your future. Managing or reducing your stress and tension responses can change your health trajectory, making you feel better both now and in the future.

HEALING STRATEGIES

After trauma, your sense of safety in the world is damaged, perhaps shattered. Healing requires reestablishing a sense of safety, both externally and internally. Rebuilding a sense of safety isn't about fooling yourself but helping your felt sense—the intersection of your internal sensations and intuitive emotional awareness—calm and align with what your mind may already realize: The danger is over. You survived. You are safe now, here in this moment and place.

To reestablish that sense of safety, let's work from the outside in.

Place

- Where do you feel most at ease? This may be your bedroom, where you've been able to decorate and surround yourself with the things and colors you like best. Or, if the trauma happened at home, it might be a place away, such as your grandmother's kitchen or a solitary place in nature.

- The things and places that bring you comfort are as unique as you are and may also be influenced by the sort of trauma you experienced. There is no right or wrong answer.

Pets

- Are there animals that help you feel calmer? As you go to or picture your peaceful place in your mind, bring those comforting beings in with you. Petting a purring cat, cuddling a warm guinea pig, or having a protective dog rest his or her chin on your knee can feel wonderful.

- Notice what happens to your heart rate and breath as you picture or interact with these companions.

Lighting

- Do you prefer bright sunlight, or dim lamplight?
- What kind of lighting makes you feel calm?

Color

- What colors soothe you? Many people find light blues and greens to be relaxing.

- Perhaps a new blanket, curtain, or painted wall might transform your personal space to one of greater serenity.

Music

- Music is another powerful mood influencer. You might be drawn to music that reflects how you feel, whether angry or tragic in sound or lyrics.

- Consider expanding your music collection to include tracks that soothe your mind and nervous system. These might be songs with sounds of nature, quiet instrumental music, or even *bilateral* music, which is specially designed to move from one ear to the other on headphones to create a soothing response. Even if these aren't your favorite tunes, having some music like this ready to use as a resource can be a wonderful tool when you need to reduce stress and anxiety.

Your body

- Consider trying yoga. Studies have proven yoga to be effective in treating trauma symptoms and in calming the nervous system. You might look for a local Trauma Sensitive Yoga class, a teen yoga class, or try an online class. The goal is not to create poses worthy of sharing on social media but to gently begin to reconnect with your physical body and breath through restorative movement and self-awareness. Graciously dismiss any negative thoughts that might discourage you as you try something new and allow yourself to rediscover what feels good and calming in your own body.

- Moving inward, consider where in your body you feel a sense of peace or even just a lack of tension. If this is difficult to find, perhaps a zone with few nerve endings, such as the cartilage of your ears or nose, might be the spot. A place associated with strength, like your hands, or grounding, such as feet, might connect with a sense of calm or well-being. This place is referred to as your *body resource* in Brainspotting therapy. When feeling stressed, anxious, or agitated, you can simply close your eyes and bring your attention to this region. Or you can keep your eyes open and find a spot to gaze at, to the left, right, center, up or down, near or far, that strengthens the sense of calm associated with your body resource because where we look changes how we feel. You might also gently lay a hand on your heart, stomach, head, or any other region where you feel tension, sending loving reassurance from your grounded part to your anxious part.

You have the strength and inner resources to heal, and you deserve this compassion.

Anxiety Assessment

How much does anxiety control your life? Use the following self-assessment to examine different ways anxiety might be showing up in your life.

	RARELY	SOMETIMES	OFTEN
I worry about things that might happen.			
I feel anxious without knowing why.			
I am scared.			
I am jumpy.			
I forget and fumble my words when talking to others.			
My mouth gets dry.			
I feel shaky.			
I find myself holding my breath or breathing shallowly.			
I have sweaty hands.			
I am careful and make sure I do things perfectly.			
I double- and triple-check things.			
I try to be prepared for everything.			
I can't get started on projects for fear of doing them wrong.			
I think of what could go wrong.			
I have trouble falling asleep.			

If you answered mostly "sometimes" or "often" to the questions in the assessment, anxiety has a moderate to strong hold on your life. You can use the tools in this book to help combat the effects.

Breath Work: Alternate Nostril Breathing

This breathing exercise comes from the practice of yoga, where it is known by the Sanskrit name *Nadi Shuddhi*, meaning "subtle energy cleansing." Focusing on the pattern of breathing clears other thoughts and worries from your mind while the breath itself oxygenates the brain, calming the nervous system.

Find a comfortable sitting position, perhaps on a cushion or stool, with your back straight and shoulders open.

Place your right thumb on your right nostril with your index and middle fingers resting between your eyebrows, and your fourth finger on your opposite nostril. Use your thumb to press gently against your nostril and take a slow inhalation through your left nostril.

Release the right nostril and close off the left with your finger, exhaling through the right nostril.

Now inhale through the right nostril, and exhale through the left.

Repeat this cycle for several minutes, ending with an exhalation through the left. When you release your hand from your face, sit for a moment and breathe naturally, noticing any changes to your breath, your body, or your feelings.

MEDITATION PRACTICE: RELEASING STRESS AND PAINFUL EMOTIONS

Find a comfortable place to sit or lie down. You can read this over and then practice it, or read it in segments, perhaps closing your eyes for a moment with each step. This can be especially helpful at the end of the day to clear your mind for sleep.

Picture yourself sitting in a shaded wood, golden light filtering through green leaves above. Before you runs a brook, burbling and splashing around stones and into an open stream that becomes a river to the sea in the distance. No one is there but you; it is calm and serene. You can smell the fresh woodsy scent.

In your hands you hold the bad feelings of today, whether guilt, shame, regret, anger, stress, worry, or fear. One by one, you take each emotion, look at it with compassion, and gently release it into the stream. Watch as it twirls in the cleansing water, then washes away. If it gets stuck on a rock or the bank, you can nudge it free with a stick, allowing it to float far away. The river only runs in one direction.

With each painful emotion you choose to release, open your hands and let it go into the clear mountain water. Wait and watch until all has floated away. Then, unburdened and light, you arise and turn, leaving it all behind.

List: Stress Reducers

You can build your resources by identifying some stress reducers that work for you personally. In the boxes that follow, list resources that work for you now or could be helpful. Don't be afraid to add ideas that you haven't tried yet.

Activities	People	Places
Music/Sounds	Smells	Other

Embracing Your Emotions

Emotions are powerful. They can lift you up in excitement, filling you with energy as you fall in love or anticipate a party, or drag you down with fear as you revisit places where scary things have happened. When you've experienced trauma, it can be tempting to try to avoid your feelings because of the intensity of the negative emotions. Unfortunately, there is no way to shut down your feelings selectively. When you push down anxiety, becoming numb, you also push away joy.

The challenge, then, is to allow yourself to feel without becoming overwhelmed. Feelings are not bad, wrong, or right; they simply are. Your feelings are valid. Even if some people around you don't seem to know how to respond, your emotions are not wrong. You don't have to make them go away.

The paradox with emotions is that the best—in fact, the only—way to truly master your emotions is to allow them; to stop wrestling with them and let yourself feel. Listen to your emotions with self-compassion and hear what they have to say.

Perhaps you've read the children's story or are familiar with the song "We're Going on a Bear Hunt." The words are repeated: "We can't go over it; we can't go under it; we've got to go through it!" And through each challenge the little adventurers go. So it is with your emotions, no matter how painful they may be. You can't skip over them. You can't skirt around them. To stop being overwhelmed by them and to heal, you must go through them and get to the other side, where healing awaits.

SOOTHING YOUR EMOTIONS

Emotions are natural responses to life. They provide immediate feedback that can help you judge a situation as positive or negative, safe or unsafe. The part of your brain that produces emotion is right at the core, connected to every other part. It developed before you developed language and thinking abilities, and it fires faster than you can even think. This gives you rapid feedback about a situation, and normally you can accept and trust your emotions or intuition as important sources of information.

Unfortunately, as we have discussed, when trauma is raw and unprocessed, your intuition becomes confused by a danger signal that keeps blaring like a useless car alarm. Because of this, it is important to give focused attention to your emotions, tune in to what they have to tell you, and decipher whether it is a true issue.

Think of your emotions as your inner puppy. Your emotions may be like a yappy dog that becomes frantic every time someone passes by on the sidewalk. Your job is to check whether the puppy's barking is due to genuine cause for alarm, and either attend to the warning or reassure the puppy. In this way you can validate the function of your feelings without being managed by them.

As you learn to accept and embrace your emotions, it is important to maintain self-awareness of your capacity. Think of it as the light dimmer switch (page 9). All the way off is generally useless, and all the way on might be overwhelming. While it's important to allow yourself to feel, recognizing your zone of emotional tolerance is key. It can help to rate your emotional intensity from zero to ten and determine what part of that range is functional for you. If you can handle emotions in the one to six range, apply grounding techniques to allow yourself to feel when you are below a one, and coping skills to regulate anything over a six. This is personal and subjective, with no right or wrong answers.

HEALING STRATEGIES

The first step to healing and handling raw emotions is awareness, followed by realistic threat assessment and self-soothing if no true danger is present. Commit to practicing the following self-care strategies daily, even when you are not in emotional crisis, so that they come to you more naturally when you need them.

Increase self-awareness through daily check-ins. Take time every day, perhaps a few times each day at regular intervals such as when waking up, coming home from school, or going to bed, to check in with yourself. Ask yourself, "What am I feeling?" Practicing this regularly will increase your self-awareness in the in-between times, too.

Try to determine the source of your feelings. Linking your emotions to the triggers or situations that influence them will grant you greater self-understanding, which can flow toward greater self-compassion. It will also help you broaden the time frame within which you notice your emotions tilting away from calm, giving you more time to respond.

Assess the situation. Is there a true or plausible threat? Do you need to take action to create or increase safety for yourself?

Take steps to soothe your frazzled or depressed emotions. Once safety is established, focus on your breath, which is one of the best and most readily accessible resources you have to soothe yourself. When anxious or threatened, people tend to hold their breath or breathe shallowly. To reassure your brain that all is well, intentionally deepen each breath and slow the rate of your breathing. Taking ten slow, deep breaths, with a slightly longer exhale than inhale, will retrain your nervous system and calm your heart and mind.

Change how you move your body to send calming signals to your brain.
Notice your posture in times of upset, and counter it with opposite movement. Do you sit rigidly? Try relaxing every muscle into a soft chair or mattress. Are you hunched forward? Throw your shoulders back and open up your chest, lifting your chin to a pose of confidence. Hold this position while you breathe and notice the change in your emotions.

Find an active pursuit you enjoy and do it regularly. Any physical activity is a stress reliever and will help build emotional resilience. Daily walks, bike rides, dancing, running, sports, kinetic video games, yoga, roller-skating, skateboarding, and swimming are all positive outlets that will relieve the buildup of stress.

REESE'S STORY

As the car pulled into the school parking lot, Reese began to feel panic. His breath came in rapid, short, painful heaves and he felt like his heart was going to beat out of his chest. He wiped his clammy hands repeatedly on his jeans and tried to keep his vision focused.

It was his first day at this school. Images filled his head of classmates surrounding him as he lay on the ground, kicking him in the head and stomach as they spat hateful insults. Reese felt like he was going to pass out. He felt frozen, wanting to run, but stuck.

"Reese," his older brother said from the driver's seat. "Reese, look at me." He waited until Reese met his eyes. "Breathe with me." Together, the brothers took slow inhales, eyes locked on one another. Even more slowly, they exhaled, and Reese pictured letting go of the memory, blowing it away with his breath. Inhale, hold, exhale, release.

"You've got this, bro," his brother said, clapping a hand on Reese's shoulder. With one last deep, shaky breath, Reese gave a wobbly grin, grabbed his backpack and, head held high, walked through the gates of his new school.

I Have a Question . . .

When I remember how the cops handcuffed and beat me when I hadn't done anything, I get so angry that I want to hurt someone! I don't think straight and I'm afraid I might do something I'll regret. What should I do?

First, it may help to understand your anger. There are multiple sources of anger, including injustice, frustration, insult, and loss of control. It sounds like your experience hit on all these. No one should ever be treated this way. Your anger is valid.

Anger also shows up when trauma activates your fight-or-flight survival instincts. When your brain's *amygdala* has prepared your body to fight, but you've used all your willpower not to because of the survival demands of the fraught situation or you can't because you're restrained, all that fighting energy remains trapped in your body.

Take some time to get in touch with your angry feelings. What's underneath them? Spend some time writing about this in a journal. To access your expressive side, try writing with your nondominant hand. This will help tap into that part of your brain.

Next, listen to what these feelings need; both the obvious feeling of anger and any more vulnerable feelings the anger is protecting. Does that trapped energy still need release? It can help to release the physical tension by going for a run or engaging in a similar nonaggressive physical activity, depending on the needs and capacity of your unique body. It's best to avoid fighting-related sports for this outlet to avoid reinforcing a connection between anger and aggression.

When you have drained the tension, be sure to follow it up with self-soothing. This is the most important part. What does the scared part need to feel safe again? Try standing in a cool shower, picturing the water washing all the fear from you, as you hold a hand to your heart and whisper the words, "You are safe now," or "It's over."

Finally, arm yourself with tools to deal with anger when it crops up. Practice slow breathing techniques that can help cool you off in the heat of the moment and regain control of your full mind and true self, who doesn't want to hurt anyone. Remind yourself that you are no longer restrained, and you can choose to walk away.

Practice: Body Scan

One of the best things you can do to gain a better understanding of and make peace with your feelings is periodic self-check-ins. One of the most effective ways to get in touch with your feelings is through your gut sense. Try this simple body scan at least once every day, or anytime you're feeling uneasy, and listen to what your body is telling you.

Close your eyes and bring your attention to your breath. Notice the flow of it gently in and out.

Now bring your attention to your body. Slowly move your awareness from your head to your neck to your shoulders to your arms. Pause anywhere you feel tension and see if there are any painful emotions connected there. Consciously relax the muscles in each part before moving on. Perhaps visualize a warm, glowing light gently melting away the tension anywhere it is found. Notice your chest, abdomen, and glutes; your thighs, calves, feet, and toes. Release any tightness you are holding in any muscles, and send loving-kindness to every cell, silently giving thanks for the work your body has done in carrying you through your day.

Calendar: My Emotion Management Plan

In the calendar spaces below, create a weekly plan for stress management and emotional release. If you participate in any regular creative or physical activities, you can start by noting those practice dates and times. Add scheduled meetings with a therapist, close friend, or other confidant. Then finish by filling in any blanks with ideas you have gleaned from this chapter.

	SUNDAY	MONDAY	TUESDAY
morning			
afternoon			
evening			

WEDNESDAY	THURSDAY	FRIDAY	SATURDAY

I give myself permission to feel and to heal.

~~~~~~~~~~~~~~~~~~~~~~~~~~~~~~~~~~~~~

I am safe in this moment.

Checklist: Soothing Strategies

There are many ways to manage stress and soothe strong emotions. Consider the following options and check off the ones that might work for you. You may want to bookmark this page for easy reference when you're feeling overwhelmed.

Pro tip: You can combine a few of these coping skills for extra effect!

☐ Write in a journal

☐ Play music

☐ Let myself cry if I feel like it

☐ Call or text a trusted friend or family member

☐ Breathe deeply

☐ Meditate or pray

☐ Draw, paint, or color something (such as a mandala)

☐ Go outside for fresh air

☐ Blow bubbles

☐ Take a cool shower or a warm bubble bath

☐ Practice yoga

☐ Dance

☐ Go for a walk or jog

☐ Bike

☐ Swim

☐ Work with clay or use a squeezy stress ball

☐ Visualize a happy or calm place (such as a favorite vacation spot)

☐ Butterfly hug (cross arms over chest and slowly tap alternating shoulders)

☐ Drink herbal tea or a glass of ice water

☐ Light a scented candle

☐ Curl up in a soft and fluffy or weighted blanket

Key Takeaways

- Emotions are neither right nor wrong—they just are.

- It is common to feel guilt or shame after trauma, but what happened was not your fault!

- Ignoring emotions doesn't make them disappear and can keep you stuck.

- Stress takes a toll on the body and mind if it is not managed.

- Increasing self-awareness helps you respond to strong emotions mindfully.

- There are many ways to handle stress, anxiety, and other strong emotions, including:

  - Physical exercise

  - Talking with trusted friends or family

  - Time with your pet

  - Letting yourself cry

  - Journaling, music, and art

  - Focused breathing, meditation, and intentional muscle relaxation

  - Sensory comforts such as baths or wrapping up in a blanket

- Most importantly, be compassionate with yourself as you allow yourself to feel.

CHAPTER 3

TAKING BACK YOUR CONTROL

Trauma impacts not only your feelings but also your thoughts and actions. All these aspects connect with and influence one another. In this chapter, you will learn ways to identify and challenge harmful thinking. You will also develop strategies to help you align your actions with what you want from life, reducing reactive behaviors that cause you further stress. This may not be easy, but one step at a time, you can do this!

Challenging the Negative

Negative thoughts seep in easily when you've been hurt. It can be tempting to blame yourself, either by thinking you caused what happened or that you somehow deserved it. You may judge yourself as negatively changed by what occurred, labeling yourself damaged or broken. You might have a darker perception of the world and the future than you once held.

The most hurtful thoughts are typically those that stem from negative beliefs about yourself. These thoughts support and maintain the painful feelings of depression or anxiety you may be experiencing. In the previous chapter, you explored many ways to cope with painful feelings. In confronting the negative beliefs that prop up those feelings, you may begin to experience some direct relief.

HEALING STRATEGIES

The first step to overcoming negative self-talk is identifying your negative thoughts. If you let yourself think of the traumatic event, what words come to mind that follow "I . . ."? Pay special attention to sentences that use all-or-nothing language, as they are probably untrue. For example, "I always mess everything up" may *feel* true but is unlikely to be accurate. Leaning into the exaggeration of your own mistakes or shortcomings will only cause you harm.

Rephrase the negative thought into something more accurate. Perhaps it is honest to admit, "I made some mistakes here."

Identify the belief you would like to hold on to regarding the situation. This should be a thought that still rings true—not fanciful thinking. However, it might be an idea that doesn't come to mind readily. "I can't trust anyone" might be replaced with "I can learn to spot the signs of trustworthy versus untrustworthy people." "I am damaged goods" might be traded for "What was done to my body did not change my worth."

Write these replacement truths as reminders. Write them on sticky notes and put them in places where you will see them regularly or use a dry-erase marker to write them on your mirror. Read these truths often until they stick. Whisper them aloud like a mantra.

Practice loving self-compassion. When you notice your thoughts moving toward the negative self-talk that has kept you stuck, be gentle with yourself. Notice where it hurts, and allow yourself to release that pain, gently using some of the coping tools you are developing. Be kind to yourself as you relearn the truth of who you are.

Don't give up on yourself. Overcoming negative self-talk takes time and practice.

Fill in the Blanks: Self-Compassion Statements

To counter negative self-talk, let's build some replacement self-compassion statements. Fill in the following blanks with words of affirmation and encouragement.

I am _____

_____.

I deserve _____

_____.

I can have _____

_____.

I learned _____

_____.

I can choose _____

_____.

I can handle _____

_____.

Table: Changing Self-Talk

Negative thoughts can be countered by finding the truth and reflecting on it in their place. The truth may not be the exact opposite, but it does address the fear or false conclusion in the negative belief. Look over the list that follows and circle the automatic negative thoughts (ANTs) that you connect with when you think of your trauma. Then highlight the replacement positive idea (ANTeater) you'd like to hold on to instead or come up with one of your own.

AUTOMATIC NEGATIVE THOUGHTS (ANTS)	ANTEATERS
It's all my fault.	I release myself from blame.
I should have done more (to escape/help others).	I survived; that was my only job. I did my best.
I could have prevented / stopped it.	I did the best I could.
I am helpless.	I have choices now.
I am a failure.	I can succeed.
I have to be perfect.	It's okay to be me.
I am not good enough.	I am enough—just as I am.
I cannot trust anyone.	I can choose who I trust.
I can't do anything right.	I am capable of many things.
I am a bad person.	I am a good person and growing.
I am worthless.	I am worthy of love.
I am forever damaged.	I can heal.
I am ugly. / I hate my body.	I accept myself and respect my body.
I don't matter.	I am important.
I can't trust myself.	I can trust my intuition and judgment.
I can't stand up for myself.	I can directly express my needs.
I can't protect myself.	I can learn to take care of myself.
I am in danger. / I'm not safe.	It's over; I am safe now.
I can't show my feelings.	I can safely express my emotions.
I can't let it out.	I can choose to open up a little bit at a time.

When you find yourself caught up in negative thinking, try this simple meditation.

First, *reflect on the good*. This can be anything completely unrelated. Look at a flower, a fluffy cloud against a blue sky, the frost pattern on your window, or your sleeping cat. Allow your mind to rest here, sweeping all other thoughts aside for the moment. Take in every aspect of that goodness. Notice the colors and patterns. Really let yourself see it and take it in.

As you do this, *notice your body*. Mindfully observe as your heart slows down, your muscles loosen, and your brow unfurrows.

Before you look away, *set an intention to remember* the good in this moment.

Finally, with the tension releasing, purposely *quiet your inner critic* and listen for wiser words of kindness. *"I can do this." "My best is good enough." "I am learning." "It will get better."*

Creating Your Narrative

When crisis hits and trauma overwhelms you, your ability to make sense of life fragments. Your memories pop up at random, and it can be hard to put together a coherent story line of what occurred. Part of healing, therefore, is constructing this sequential, comprehensive narrative. This process allows you to package up and hold what feels wild and unruly: that which refuses to fit neatly in a box and be filed away as history.

This might sound simple enough, but perhaps you feel some apprehension at a gut level. Your instinct is not wrong: This is no simple task. Allowing yourself to remember it all takes true courage. So go slowly. Allow yourself to feel, to cry, to release everything as you go along. If you find yourself feeling "floaty" and disconnected from yourself, ground yourself using your five senses.

You don't have to complete this all at once. Stay tuned in to your emotional needs, and return to your coping skills as often as you need.

GETTING STARTED

There is more than one way to create a narrative. You may find writing in a journal a good outlet and way to organize your thoughts and memories. Perhaps writing isn't your thing but recording voice memos or videos is. Drawing your story as cartoons or portraits and later placing the images in order works for some. Others simply tell their story with words, talking it through from beginning to end with a trusted listener such as a therapist, relative, or friend.

Don't place an expectation on yourself to get it all out at once. Write, walk away, let yourself feel. Pay attention to what your body is telling you. Release what comes up through physical movement and breath. Come back to it another day. You can start over at the beginning with a fresh perspective or pick up again where you left off. You'll likely find that the content of what you write shifts as you heal and gain new perspectives.

Resist the temptation to write in the third person (talking about yourself as she, he, they, etc.). This separates you from the emotions, which feels safer, but blocks you from the powerful processing of the trauma that this exercise can bring. Tune into all your senses as you tell your story, noting what you saw, felt, heard, smelled, and sensed.

If you are using video to record your story, be cautious about sharing it on social media while it is still raw. Remember the truth that *the internet is forever* and think carefully about whether you are sure Future You will be as comfortable as Present You is with putting it all out there. Additionally, the pressures of creating a social-media-ready video will distract from the goals of healing, as your awareness of what others might think will naturally reorient you from the internal focus needed to truly process. While you certainly have no reason to be ashamed and do not need to hide, worrying about harsh feedback from those who don't understand isn't what you need right now. No one gets to judge your pain.

Whatever your process, this work is for you. Take your time with it and follow the process that fits you best.

HEALING STRATEGIES

As you begin to piece together the narrative of your trauma, you will inevitably feel one of two things, or possibly both. You might feel disconnected from any sense or feeling as you factually lay out the events. While this might seem ideal, such dissociation from the emotion suggests you are not getting all the benefits of deeply processing your trauma through this work. But this is still of value, as you can later use your recorded narrative to share with your therapist, or to reflect on each part to help you get in touch with what you felt as it occurred. In this case, you're creating a foundational stepping-stone to healing.

Alternatively, you may feel emotionally raw as you construct your narrative, like you are poking an unhealed wound. You might feel shame, anger, fear, revulsion, or other intense discomfort, and notice your stomach clenching, a knot in your throat, your heart pounding, or your muscles becoming tense. This can lead to dissociation to escape the pain, or simply leave you overwhelmed by distress.

It is important for healing that you feel but not become retraumatized. There is a zone of optimal emotion between numbness and flooding. If you feel overwhelmed in the creation of your personal narrative:

- Stop and take a break.

- Check in with yourself as you do this work and give yourself permission to pause.

- Close the journal, turn off the recording, put down the pencil or markers.

- Drink some water.

- Go outside.

- Breathe.

There is always time for self-care, and there will always be more time to heal.

VIKRAM'S STORY

"I wrote something," Vikram mumbled as he plopped himself down on his therapist's couch. His eyes darted up nervously to meet his therapist's, gazing back with a gentle mix of patience and curiosity. "Um, can I read it?"

"I'd love to hear it," his therapist replied.

Vikram paused and fidgeted with the paper, clearing his throat and tapping his toe nervously. Finally he began. In an expressionless voice he read from the folded paper, afraid to meet his therapist's eyes. Sometimes he paused, the lump in his throat too large to go on. Still, his therapist waited patiently. "Take your time, Vikram."

When he got to the end, Vikram folded the paper again and finally lifted his eyes, searching his therapist's face. "Wow…" she said gently, her face full of compassion. "Thank you for sharing this with me. That was really brave."

For the first time, Vikram had spoken aloud his deeply buried secret. It was one of the scariest things he'd done: he was so afraid he'd be condemned as dirty and bad. But the compassion and validation he received instead was like helium to his spirits. He felt lighter, freer, and more sure of himself than he had in a very long time.

Reflection Prompts

If you are having trouble getting started as you begin to sort your thoughts to tell your story, the following questions might help. But know that there is no right or wrong way to tell your very personal narrative, so don't feel constrained by these prompts.

- What is the title of your story?

- What happened first?

- What were you thinking, doing, feeling, and imagining at the time?

- How did you respond?

- How did it end?

- How did you know it was over?

- What are the stories (interpretations) you tell yourself about the trauma?

- How does this history impact your life today?

- What have you learned about yourself, or how have you grown?

- What positive characteristics does the protagonist (you) possess?

- Having completed the telling or writing of your story, does the title still apply, or would you change it somehow?

- What might the next story line of your life be?

I Have a Question . . .

I've been trying to write about what happened to me, but I keep feeling like I am writing about someone else. I even start to feel like I'm not real. What should I do?

What you are describing is dissociation. This is your brain's way of protecting you when something becomes emotionally overwhelming. To counteract this, bring yourself back to the present through grounding techniques.

Grounding happens when you use your senses to reconnect to your body, to the present, and to where you are. Begin by pressing your feet firmly into the ground, paying attention to the connection between your feet and the floor. Notice the fabrics of your clothing against your skin, the firmness or softness of your chair. Splash cool water on your face. Sing along to music or use your voice in some other audible way. Notice where your eyes want to lock and purposefully move them to other things at varying distances and angles, naming what you see. Select as few or as many of these tools as you need to remind yourself of who you are, where you are, and how old you are—and that the danger is over. You are safe now.

MEDITATION PRACTICE: HEALING POOL

Settle into a comfortable position, sitting or lying down. Bring your attention to your breathing, filling your lungs slowly and even more slowly releasing. As you read the following guided meditation, take time to pause and visualize, perhaps closing your eyes after each paragraph to immerse yourself in the scene.

You are walking through a verdant green rain forest. Light trickles down through the lush canopy of leaves overhead. The sounds of birds calling are a peaceful music to your ears. As you listen, you hear a faint splashing sound, and move in that direction.

You come upon an opening in the trees, where a small pool has formed at the bottom of a little waterfall. You sit down at the edge, removing your shoes. There's something different about this pool; you can sense it. Perhaps it is something in its enticing fragrance.

You decide to dip your feet in the water and find it to be surprisingly, pleasantly warm. You notice that the tension in your tired feet instantly begins to ease, your muscles relaxing. You consider whether to immerse yourself farther. You can see the bottom of the pool through the clear, turquoise blue and notice its gentle slope, allowing you to safely control your entrance and depth.

As you ease into the warm, clear water, you feel all negative thoughts washing off you and away. Every fear, every sense of limitation, every feeling of shame somehow dissolves in this magical pool as its waters detoxify and rejuvenate your mind, body, and spirit. Noticing how much lighter and freer you feel, you might linger here, floating, resting, and soaking in the beauty and warmth. Stay as long as you like, washing away all that doesn't serve you.

Reframing Your Mindset

Negative thinking can take different forms, known as *cognitive distortions*. One common pitfall comes from a sense of hopelessness. This can lead to pessimistic *fortune-telling*, or *catastrophizing* (assuming the worst will happen). Negative thinking can also take the form of *discounting the positive* to focus only on the negatives, *overgeneralizing* negative experiences as though they will happen everywhere with everyone, or *all-or-nothing* thinking in which only a perfect solution is acceptable. You may fall into the trap of *personalization* of negative events, causing you to blame yourself where blame is not appropriate. This may lead to *labeling*, wherein you may call yourself names rather than simply accepting an isolated mistake for what it is. It is easy to fall in the trap of *should*s, which keeps you ensnared in guilt and stress. These cognitive biases naturally keep you stuck in a dark headspace.

To escape these traps, let's look at some concrete ways to reframe negative thoughts and break free of harmful thinking.

ELIMINATING THE NEGATIVE

A pattern of negative thinking will erode your happiness, leading you into and trapping you in depression and anxiety. Many automatic negative thoughts will naturally resolve as the traumas they stem from are reprocessed at a deep, multisensory level in therapy. Nevertheless, there is much that you can do to take control of these patterns and their connection to your moods. Feelings impact our thoughts, but thoughts also shape our feelings. Addressing the negative cycle at any point will produce benefits.

The first step to breaking the cycle of negative thoughts is to notice and identify the patterns. Familiarize yourself with the different patterns of negative thinking described in the previous section and watch for signs of these pitfalls in your own inner world. It may help to keep a log, perhaps using the exercises that follow, to analyze the thought spirals that connect to your bad feelings.

As you become aware of the fallacies in your thought processes, bring self-compassion to the struggle and gently confront your negative beliefs. For instance, if you find yourself thinking "Guys are all dangerous predators; I'll never trust any again" (an example of an overgeneralization), pause and consider whether that statement can be modified while still honoring the truth of your experience with one guy (or more). It might be truer to say, "Mike was a dangerous predator. I can learn the red flags of guys like him and be cautious of whom to trust in the future."

Or perhaps you catch yourself engaging in pessimistic fortune-telling, such as "Everyone is going to hate me." Because you obviously can't know this, a more honest assessment might be "Not everyone will like me, but that's okay; I am likable and can find those with whom I have things in common."

MINDFULNESS PRACTICE: BUBBLES

As you firmly but gently confront your negative thought patterns, it's time to learn to let go. Notice the obsessive worries, the catastrophizing, the labels, the *shoulds*—all the harmful thought patterns your mind traces—and visualize letting them go. Picture placing each negative thought in a bubble as you inhale, and exhale, gently blowing the bubble and the thought away. Imagine it floating up and far, far away. You might even do this with an actual bubble-blowing wand, visualizing each literal bubble filled with your ANTs. Then bring yourself back to something good that you can hear, feel, or see in your present surroundings.

Fill in the Blanks: Rewriting Negative Thoughts

Practice redirecting negative thinking patterns by changing the following negative thoughts into neutral interpretations.

Jumping to conclusions: *They didn't speak to me when I walked in the classroom. They must be mad at me.*

Neutral interpretation: _____

Fortune-telling/catastrophizing: *I'm going to forget my speech and make a fool of myself.*

Neutral interpretation: _____

Overgeneralizing: *That dog bit me; dogs are vicious.*

Neutral interpretation: _____

All-or-nothing thinking: *I'll never get my room cleaned before I leave for practice; there's no point in even starting.*

Neutral interpretation: _____

Personalization: *The cat wouldn't sit on my lap. Even my pet hates me.*

Neutral interpretation: _____

Labeling: *I screwed up again; I'm such an idiot.*

Neutral interpretation: _____

*Should*s: *I should be able to handle this.*

Neutral interpretation:_____

Table: Tracking My Changing Thoughts

Now that you have some familiarity with common cognitive distortions, let's make it personal. Use the boxes that follow to fill in examples from your own life when you've fallen into these mental traps, and write a corrective idea for each one.

TYPE OF COGNITIVE DISTORTION	EXAMPLE FROM MY LIFE	ALTERNATIVE THOUGHTS
Jumping to conclusions		
Mental filtering		
Catastrophizing		
Overgeneralizing		
All-or-nothing thinking		
Personalization		
Labeling		
Shoulds		

Checklist: Accepting What I Can't Control

Check the items that are under your control. Notice what is left unchecked. Practice letting these things go and shifting focus to where you have power.

- ☐ How much homework I get
- ☐ If the person I ask out says yes
- ☐ How I manage my time
- ☐ Whether I have nightmares
- ☐ What I say
- ☐ What time I go to bed
- ☐ How I react to my friends
- ☐ My parent's mood
- ☐ Who I spend time with
- ☐ What I eat
- ☐ The volume of my voice
- ☐ If I'm invited to the party
- ☐ What music I listen to

- ☐ If others gossip
- ☐ Whether to play a sport
- ☐ What electives to take
- ☐ Who to confide in
- ☐ Whether others follow through
- ☐ How much time to spend on social media
- ☐ Who I follow on social media
- ☐ How many people like my posts
- ☐ The past
- ☐ Plans and goals for my life after high school
- ☐ How I calm myself

Examining Your Triggers

The word *trigger* is thrown around a lot these days. Too often it is used as an insult. But do you know what a trigger actually is?

A trigger is something in the present that reminds a trauma survivor in an acute and vivid way of their trauma, causing a flashback or internal sensation of reexperiencing some aspect of what happened. You might experience your heart suddenly pounding, your face becoming flushed, or your hands trembling. You may be thrown into fight, flight, or freeze mode and become highly reactive to the present scenario, though the true danger was in the past. A trigger makes the past feel immediate and the present threatening.

While you can't prevent triggers, you can manage them by identifying what your personal triggers are, increasing awareness of your reactivity, and planning soothing strategies.

WHAT CAN BE A TRIGGER?

Anything can be a trigger. Triggers are connected to your trauma in some sensory or thematic way and are as personal as your experience. Someone who experienced an attack near a Christmas tree may be triggered into flashbacks of the attack when smelling a pine air freshener. Someone who was mauled by a dog may be triggered by the sound of barking while survivors of mass shootings frequently react to the explosive sounds of fireworks. The sight of flashing lights on an emergency vehicle could be triggering to someone whose trauma involved police or another emergency response. When trauma is relational, similar interaction styles can also be triggering. For example, someone walking away during a conflict could trigger painful memories of a parent walking out of the house and never returning and create panicky feelings of abandonment.

Understanding your own triggers is an important part of healing. When you notice yourself having a strong reaction to something, observe it with open curiosity. Perhaps revisit times you've become angry, scared, or flooded, and explore what happened just before. What were you feeling? Close your eyes and sit with that emotion for a moment. Allow yourself to float back in your mind to a time when you felt that way before. Consider the earliest time you can remember feeling like that. This will allow you to connect the dots of your trauma, your triggers, and your reactions. Then picture the calm version of your present self, extending compassion to that hurt inner version of yourself.

HEALING STRATEGIES

Knowing what your triggers are—both what sets you off and what it is linked to—is essential to healing. When triggered, notice your bodily reaction. Recognize that your reaction in the present is magnified because it is reflecting the past. Validate to yourself how real your feelings are while reminding yourself that the trauma is over. You are safe now.

This is not time for self-condemnation or harsh self-talk. Triggers are an unfortunate but normal part of trauma while you are still healing. Be compassionate with yourself and consider what you need to move through this intense, painful moment. Consider what kinds of self-care strategies might be helpful.

Deep breathing. Begin by inhaling slowly through your nose while you count to four, and exhaling even more slowly with a count to six. Repeat this while you stay mindfully aware of the beat of your heart, the feel of your skin, and the tension of your muscles.

Sensory grounding. Use your senses to ground yourself to the present, gently pulling yourself away from the reminders of the past into the safety of now. Look around you and identify four blue things you see, three sounds you hear, two things you can feel, and something you smell. Notice where you are. Tune into your sense of your body, and notice your height, your strength, and your freedom. Move your body in ways that reinforce these truths.

Writing down your triggers. Jot down any experiences that have caused you to feel triggered. These highlight key points where the trauma can be powerfully reprocessed in therapy with EMDR or Brainspotting. Noting your triggers helps to get to the heart of the trauma. You don't have to be ashamed of, nor do you need to suppress, your triggers. They are merely signposts highlighting the path to follow toward freedom.

I Have a Question . . .

In 2020, I got COVID and had to stay in the hospital. No one could visit me, the medical staff looked inhuman under all their protective medical gear, and I was so scared I was going to die in there all alone. Now, whenever I have to go to the doctor or dentist, I feel trapped and panicky, like I can't breathe all over again. My dads say I still have to go to the appointments, but to me, it's just not worth it. What should I do?

What a frightening experience! It's no wonder you are triggered by medical environments. It's good that you can identify the link between your medical trauma and your present symptoms. Understanding is half the battle. When you face a medical appointment, remind yourself that the scary feelings are from your history, and that the panic symptoms won't last. That knowledge alone can be reassuring.

Avoiding medical appointments could lead to further problems and suffering you don't need, so, with deep compassion, I'm with your dads on this one. However, you don't have to suffer without resources. Try grounding techniques and reassuring self-talk to remind yourself that you are no longer in a quarantined hospitalization, the danger has passed, and you are going to be okay. Play music or listen to a guided meditation on headphones while waiting at the doctor's office. Notice where your gaze is fixed and choose to look in an opposite direction. Notice your body posture and sit up straight to give your lungs more space, then slow and deepen your breath with loving intention. It's not easy when you must face your triggers, but as you courageously do so, armed with coping skills, you may find that the tension lessens a little more with each visit.

Chart: My Triggers

Recognizing your triggers is the first step to reducing their control in your life. Use this chart to note what triggers you. You can bring these notes to your trauma therapist to desensitize each hot point one by one.

Sounds	
Sights	
Smells	
Sensations	
Other	

Checklist: Grounding Techniques

When you are triggered, a sensory cue catapults you from the present to the past where the trauma lies. Look over this list of grounding techniques and check off those that might be helpful to you in such a moment. Then bookmark or copy this page to keep handy for when you need a reminder.

☐ Remember the date, your age, and your location. Say them aloud.

☐ Remind yourself: "I am safe now," or "It is over."

☐ Take slow, deep breaths.

☐ Drink a cold glass of water.

☐ Drink a carbonated beverage. Notice the flavor, the coolness, and how the fizz pops against your nose.

☐ Chew gum. Pay attention to the flavor and the muscles in your jaw.

☐ Spray some air freshener, cologne, or perfume. Try to distinguish the scents.

☐ Light a candle on a sturdy surface. Watch the flame and smell the fragrance.

☐ Listen for three distinct sounds in your environment, near or distant.

☐ Play music (bilateral or other). Bonus: sing, drum, or dance along.

☐ Find three things of different textures and feel them, noting the different sensations.

☐ Wrap yourself in a soft or weighted blanket.

☐ Turn on a fan or open a window, noticing the cool air on your skin.

☐ Take a cool shower or splash water on your face. Pay attention to the sensation.

☐ Look for five things that are your favorite color.

☐ Touch five things that are circular.

☐ Stand up and stretch. Notice anywhere you feel tense or sore.

☐ Balance on one foot, then the other.

☐ Interact with your pet.

☐ Take your shoes off and press your feet into the ground. Bonus: do this outside in grass or soil.

Reacting Constructively

Every behavior has a reason, and harmful behaviors stem from wounds or unmet needs. So often those who have been traumatized act in ways that appear rebellious or are otherwise judged as character defects. Such behaviors, while not without meaning, do cause secondary struggles and often have long-term consequences. To avoid this additional suffering, let's take a look at some common pitfalls, the links to trauma, and ways to reduce falling into these traps by meeting your needs constructively instead.

BEHAVING RECKLESSLY

The emotional pain, heightened reactivity, and existential questions resulting from trauma can show up in many harmful ways. It is common for trauma survivors of all ages to turn to substance use to try to numb the pain and blur the vividness of intrusive memories. Unfortunately, this is like trying to dig yourself out of a pit: The more you use, the worse the emotional turmoil becomes. Some survivors use substances to try to fall asleep when anxiety keeps them hyperalert, not realizing that substances such as alcohol and marijuana change the quality of sleep. Because deep sleep and dream cycles are an essential component of our brain's natural remedy to stress, trauma symptoms become more deeply entrenched through this maladaptive coping cycle. Additionally, these act as depressants, causing the brain to cycle into increasingly darker moods in between use. The pain and need for relief are real, but the response is problematic.

Survivors of sexual trauma tend to react behaviorally in one of two ways, either self-protectively closing down to physical touch or becoming hypersexual in ways that can make them vulnerable to further trauma and regrets. You may be following the *all-or-nothing* cognitive distortion that because someone has "had sex" with you, it doesn't matter anymore whether you have sex with anyone, or believe the lie that you are "damaged goods," or have no right to say no to anyone. You might become dissociative when triggered by sexual innuendo and find yourself in a *freeze* or *fawn* mode where you go through the motions with anyone who initiates because resisting was futile in the past. Or you may seek to reclaim power over your sexuality by choosing (even with little desire) to be sexual rather than have it taken from you. You may have never really considered why you do the things you do, and brush off judgment and labels you unfairly receive. But behavior that is followed subconsciously is neither free nor empowered. What is not enthusiastically consented to is likely to become a secondary trauma wound. You deserve to heal and find the freedom to make choices that feel right to you at every level—body, soul, and spirit.

Some trauma survivors gain a bad reputation from skipping school or appearing to no longer care about grades. Underneath the apparent disengagement, difficulty concentrating due to intrusive memories, flashbacks, and poor sleep may be causing frustration and lowered grades while hopelessness about the future may make the efforts seem meaningless. These symptoms are real and understandable barriers. And yet, struggling without help now can derail your future and your very real potential in significant ways. If you notice your trauma is leading to these outcomes, you are *not* a failure. It is, however, time to ask for help to heal the heart of the problem.

In addition to academic consequences, feeling hopeless about the future and like nothing matters, or feeling numb and seeking out something to make you feel alive again can lead down many self-destructive paths, from self-harm to thrill-seeking criminal behaviors. Anger at the world may add fuel to this dangerous fire. Anger turned inward harms you while anger turned outward harms both you and others. But underneath that anger or the numbness that seeks to feel alive, what feelings are suppressed? Allowing yourself to get in touch with these feelings and compassionately moving through them will eventually reduce the need to act in ways that cause you harm.

You are a good person, but a hurting person. Let the hurt heal so that the goodness shines through.

HEALING STRATEGIES

To truly be in charge of your life and avoid behavior patterns that send your life hurtling further from your control, learn to move through the world with mindfulness. Mindfulness is full awareness in the present moment, not only of what is around you, but of what is within. Living mindfully empowers you to act intentionally, with full awareness of the reasons you are choosing and the potential outcomes of your choice.

Mindfulness requires you to look inside, where the pain resides. This is not easy. You don't have to do it all at once or to stay there immersed in the pain.

- Give yourself space to remember and to feel, just a little bit at a time.

- Visualize placing all the memories and their hurt in a container, sealing it up, and tucking it away until next time.

- Use the soothing strategies you learned in chapter 2 to fortify yourself as you do the hard work of self-compassion.

- When facing temptation, ask yourself, "Is this really what I want?" You are no longer a victim. You have control in this moment. You have the power and freedom to choose what truly feels right, and what will be good for you both now and in your future.

KRIS'S STORY

Fourteen-year-old Kris hadn't been the same since the bullet zipped through her bedroom, making a small hole through the wall right over her bed. Though she and her family were unhurt, she couldn't shake the newfound awareness that life could be over in a flash.

School felt meaningless. If she had no assurance that she would live to see graduation, why waste hours studying? Why put off until adulthood things she might never get to experience should another incident happen, and this time claim her life?

Everyone condemned her experiments with alcohol, sex, and partying. She overheard a teacher refer to her as a delinquent. But Kris wasn't a bad kid—she just didn't want to miss out! What was the point of playing by the rules if the rules couldn't guarantee anything?

Kris's heart pounded with excitement as she snuck her mom's car from the garage late one night. Her friends waited at the corner as she rolled up with the headlights off. As they peeled out of the neighborhood, the music was blaring and their laughter bright. They didn't see the police until the red and blue lights flashed in the rearview mirror.

Waiting nervously in the station for her mom to arrive, Kris realized there was more than one way to lose her future. She decided it was time to face the past and find a way to live well in the present.

I Have a Question . . .

I know that it's not good for me in the long term and that I could get in trouble for it because I'm underage, but I can't relax and fall asleep if I don't smoke first. I'm just too tense. What can I do?

That is such an understandable struggle. And you're right, using marijuana over the long term does lead to patterns of increased anxiety between usage and exponentially increases your risk of developing a psychotic disorder when used in adolescence, and some research suggests it shrinks your brain. Yet, sleep is so important.

A few alternatives you might try include deep breathing before bed, visualizing yourself in a calm, happy place, or progressive muscle relaxation, where you focus on each muscle group from your head to your toes, tensing and then relaxing each muscle. You might also try visualizing putting your stresses in a container until tomorrow or sweeping the thoughts from your mind with an imaginary broom.

Exercising and getting outside in bright sunlight earlier in the day and keeping a consistent bedtime will also help to cue your brain and body to sleep. A cup of herbal tea or a light protein snack can also be a helpful bedtime routine. If you continue to struggle, you might consider over-the-counter remedies such as melatonin but be careful not to use this over the long term, either. If nightmares are part of your struggle, a doctor might prescribe *prazosin* to help improve your sleep. Finally, working through your trauma in therapy is likely to produce dramatic changes in your ability to sleep. Know that there are many tools available. You have the power to make change!

List: Healthy Coping Strategies

When feeling drawn toward self-destructive habits that you'd like to end, consider the strategies you might use instead. You can break the cycle and choose a path of self-care.

☐ Wait a day—give yourself time to reflect before deciding.

☐ Ask yourself why you want to do it. What need is it meeting?

☐ Explore alternate ways to meet that need, such as:

- Write about your feelings.
- Listen to music.
- Talk to a trusted friend or adult.
- Ask to see a therapist or counselor.
- Try a physical outlet such as biking or yoga to release stress.
- Create something.
- (Add your own.)

_____

_____

_____

_____

Chart: Problem-Solving

Use the chart that follows to reduce reliance on unhealthy coping strategies. Seek input from trusted adults if you need help thinking of strategies.

BEHAVIOR	THOUGHTS	FEELINGS	NEED	ALTERNATIVE WAYS TO MEET NEED
Example: Cutting my arm	I don't matter	Numb	To feel alive & connected	- Take a cool shower - Text a friend - Pet the cat - Walk the dog

PRACTICE: VICTORIOUS BREATHING

No matter the stressor you are facing, the negative thoughts, or the temptations, returning to your breath with intentional focus is always a good way to ground, center, and calm yourself. This breathing exercise is called *Ujjayi* breath, which in Sanskrit means "conquering" or "victorious breath." As you begin to reclaim control in your spirit and your life, use this breath to conquer anxieties and become victorious, allowing it to calm you from the inside out.

Find a comfortable upright sitting position. Straighten your back and open your shoulders to allow your lungs full movement.

Take a slow, deep breath in through your nose, feeling the cool air traveling in.

Exhale long and slow through your mouth, slightly constricting the back of your throat to make a gentle "ha" sound as you exhale. Empty your lungs completely.

Take another full inhale through your nose, and exhale through your mouth, perhaps breathing onto your raised hand to feel your exhaling breath.

Inhale through your nose. Exhale, picturing fogging up a window or mirror with the warmth of your breath.

As you continue to inhale and exhale at your own slow and steady pace, picture writing a word with your finger in the fog your exhale creates—a word of kindness and affirmation to your inner self. Even as it fogs over with your continued breathing, know that the truth of it remains, strong and steady.

I choose to believe in myself.

I am resourceful, capable, and strong.

Key Takeaways

- Trauma fragments your experience.

- Putting the pieces together in a chronological narrative helps to heal this fragmentation.

- Notice the sensations and release the feelings this process brings up through movement.

- Negative beliefs are common after trauma.

- You can break patterns of negative thinking by noticing the mental traps and rewriting the script.

- Triggers are cues from your environment that bring back the feelings or memories of trauma.

- Grounding techniques can help you soothe triggered reactions.

- All behavior has meaning, even self-destructive behavior.

- Understanding the reasons for your own behavior empowers you to choose consciously.

- You deserve a good life now and a good future—be kind to Future You in the choices you make today!

CHAPTER 4

DEVELOPING RESILIENCY

You have expanded your understanding of trauma, begun to develop ways to cope and deal with the intense emotions trauma brings, and addressed the negative beliefs that have held you down. You are well on your way to healing!

As you move forward on your healing path, you continue to live and face new challenges. A history of trauma can make it more difficult to weather new storms. Novel challenges and hurts can trigger old fears and pain and lead to a rebound of anxious or depressed emotions.

On the other hand, finding meaning and purpose in the face of life-shattering experiences can lead to *post-traumatic growth*, or the ability to grow and thrive after traumatic circumstances. In this chapter, you will explore ways to build your personal resilience, or your ability to adapt and not succumb in turbulent times, and perhaps even to reach toward post-traumatic growth.

Unpacking Resilience

Resilience isn't absence of struggle, difficulty, or distress. Rather, resiliency develops bit by bit, as you create and practice strategies for coping with hurdles, maintaining emotional equilibrium, and elevating contentment and self-confidence. The greater your resilience, the greater your control within your own life and in the situations you face. Developing resiliency helps ward off and minimize depression, anxiety, frustration, and stress.

Keep in mind that no matter what skills you develop, depression, anxiety, and triggered reactions are *not* failure. These are understandable reactions to overwhelming or unhealed life stresses and traumas. Please do not mistake this chapter as carrying any hint of blame or condemnation if you continue to, or again in the future, experience mental health struggles. Resilience work will reduce your susceptibility to such struggles, not make you immune. The best approach involves both deep trauma healing and then resilience practices as a protective layer. Resilience strategies are like sunscreen that reduces, but can't fully prevent, your likelihood of sunburn or skin damage, enabling you to enjoy all that life has to offer more freely.

HEALING STRATEGIES

Cultivate self-compassion. This is the first and most important step in building resilience. If you regard yourself with loving-kindness, allowing only respect and compassion from your inner voice, you become your own ally. Avoiding negative self-talk means facing struggles without an inner bully compounding the stress.

Avoid pessimistic and catastrophizing thought patterns. Be on alert for this type of thinking so that you can firmly but respectfully dismiss worst-case scenarios. Instead, try to stay in the present, focusing on what is and the known challenges. This empowers you to direct your energy to addressing that over which you have some control. It also decreases the amount of distress you experience.

Remain in the present. By bravely addressing challenges as they come without beating yourself up or succumbing to "I can't" beliefs, you will find it easier to come to a place of acceptance.

Determine what you have control over. Putting your personal power into practice in these arenas makes it easier to accept that there are some things you simply can't change.

Allow yourself to grieve losses. Moving through adolescence means many big life changes, and with change come new opportunities and freedoms as well as loss. Acknowledge and mourn the losses while savoring the good times. Reminisce and hold on to gratitude as you navigate change. Holding this good within you will fortify you with the strength and courage to face change.

Practice gratitude. A daily dose of gratitude will lift you up and help you find hope and happiness in the ordinary. At the end of each day, list in a journal things for which you are grateful. Soon you may find yourself looking for the good so you'll have something to write, and so adopt a mindfully positive spirit.

Find meaning and purpose in your struggles and in the greater experience of life. This is a key component of resilience. Whether it takes the shape of a traditional faith or religion, or something more personal and esoteric, finding significance will pull you forward. As you make meaning and find your own way to contribute to the world, you may find yourself increasingly grounded and rooted in connection to the planet, other creatures, and humankind.

Build your support system. A solid support system with healthy, boundary-fortified interdependence is a critical aspect of fostering resilience.

ISABELLA'S STORY

Her parents' divorce had been a huge adjustment for Isabella. It had all happened so fast: the announcement, selling the home, the moves to two separate apartments. At only five years old, she hadn't seen it coming; hadn't known how to cope.

Now fifteen, Isabella is consciously working on letting herself trust people rather than closing herself off for fear of abandonment. When she looks back on her five-year-old self, she can see beyond that horrible night when her world had come crashing down. She remembers the big backyard with fondness and has gratitude in her heart that she lived on that quiet street while learning to ride her bicycle. She thinks of the present, and smiles, thinking of the friends she's made through the swim team. If she hadn't had to move, she might never have met them. Outside her window, Isabella watches a squirrel peek in from the branches of the tall green tree that shades her room. Sometimes even the little things are enough to make her smile.

I Have a Question . . .

My family lost everything in the flood. Our home was destroyed and every-
thing in it. We had to move, so I lost all my friends and teachers, too. How
am I supposed to be grateful when I've lost everything?

What a tremendous amount of loss! Forcing gratitude in the face of such
trauma and tragedy is unhelpful and unhealthy. You need to be able to grieve for
all you've lost. Acknowledge your pain and sorrow and allow yourself to feel all
the feelings that come with that. As you move through this grief, a space for gratitude will gradually emerge. Don't force it. Just be open to it. As you are ready,
begin to look for the good around you. Perhaps it will show its face in awareness
of your health, your family, your abilities, nature, new opportunities, and hope for
your future. It might emerge as quietly, subtly, and fleetingly as a rainbow. Just
be open to the good. Allow yourself to truly absorb it when you find it. Gratitude
will grow.

Checklist: Resiliency

Assess your current resiliency with this checklist. How many statements are true right now? Which areas need work? Come back to this list again in a couple of months and see how much has changed. You can grow your capacity for resilience.

- ☐ I have friends I call on when I'm upset.
- ☐ There are some adults I trust.
- ☐ People in my life encourage or help me when I need it.
- ☐ I feel connected to others.
- ☐ My family supports me.
- ☐ I know how to resolve conflict.
- ☐ I have goals.
- ☐ My life has a sense of purpose.
- ☐ Life has a sense of meaning.
- ☐ I can think of things that are good in my life.
- ☐ I know that I will be okay when things change.
- ☐ I am flexible and adaptable.
- ☐ I can express my feelings.
- ☐ I'm not afraid to cry.

- ☐ I can calm myself in crisis.
- ☐ I know that I am capable.
- ☐ I am a problem solver.
- ☐ I am independent yet can work cooperatively.
- ☐ I set boundaries when things don't feel good.
- ☐ When things go wrong, I don't automatically blame myself.
- ☐ When things go wrong, I don't automatically blame others.
- ☐ Even when things go wrong, I can imagine positive outcomes.
- ☐ I have a sense of humor.
- ☐ My inner voice is kind.
- ☐ I am confident in who I am.
- ☐ I can see ways I have grown and become stronger due to things I've gone through.

Fill in the Blanks: Gratitude

Find a notebook to use as a gratitude journal. It doesn't have to be anything fancy, just a dedicated place to list your thoughts. Keep it by your bed or somewhere you'll see it as part of your evening routine. Before you turn out the light each night, spend some time reflecting on your favorite part of the day. This can be especially challenging on hard days, but that is when it is needed most. Then, list at least one thing, trying to work your way up to three daily, that you appreciated that day. To get started, reflect on the following thoughts:

- Someone I'm thankful for: _____

- A good thing that happened today: _____

- The best thing I ate today: _____

- Something beautiful I saw today: _____

- I'm so glad that I have: _____

- Somewhere I'm glad I could be today: _____

- I'm so glad that I am: _____

- Something that made me smile today: _____

Practice: Appreciating the World around You

To practice mindful appreciation, go outside for a walk, sit outside, gaze out a window, or simply use the environment you're currently in. Look around, tuning your attention to really notice. Find one thing that is lovely: a buzzing bee, a tall tree, an intricate pattern on fabric, the way that dust dances in streams of light in late afternoon. Turn all your attention for a few moments to that one thing. Notice its movement, any sound it makes, its color, shape, and size. Notice the way you feel inside as you take time to pause and appreciate what you're observing. Take a moment to hold gratitude in your heart or to offer a little prayer, if that is part of your spiritual practice, before moving on.

Fostering Your Wellness Routine

After experiencing trauma, maintaining emotional health can be challenging. One way to create optimal conditions for your mental health to grow and recover is by creating consistency. There may be areas of your life where you don't have or haven't had control, and this unpredictability can be destabilizing. Developing a routine that fosters wellness can rebuild some of this much-needed stability. Consider the things that make you feel your best, help you cope with stress, and are consistent with your values, and develop a plan to embed these in your life regularly. As you make these things a practice, you create the conditions for both healing and resilience to develop.

FINDING PURPOSE

What brings you joy? What comforts you? What activities energize you? What brings meaning and purpose to your life?

As you reflect on these questions, you will begin to see a road map to well-being take shape. This will be as individual as you are and can incorporate hobbies, passions, interests, beliefs, and goals.

Spiritual beliefs and practices are meaningful aspects of life for many. In research I conducted on surviving mass shootings, I found that, for many people of faith, leaning into their spirituality brought a sense of meaning and comfort after catastrophe while, for others, reconciling their experience with their faith or shifting beliefs was a critical challenge to navigate in moving forward. Regardless of faith or religion, the process of making meaning is a crucial component of *post-traumatic growth*. This may simply mean finding ways to live out important values, such as trying to make the world a better place, caring for others, or connecting with the earth. Prioritizing your spirituality and practicing your values can grow your resilience.

HEALING STRATEGIES

There isn't a one-size-fits-all answer to creating the best wellness routine. There are, however, some essentials to include.

Movement. Make sure your routine includes a form of movement that works for your unique body. Trauma remains trapped in the body, and movement allows you to free it. Movement also helps to ground and connect you to your body, reducing dissociation. It can distract you from disturbing thoughts, remind you of your capability and strength, and build a sense of agency or control. Exercise releases *endorphins*, which are happiness hormones that fortify you against everyday stressors. Physical activity increases your levels of *serotonin, norepinephrine,* and *dopamine*, which are all natural antidepressants. Serotonin is especially important for good sleep. Finally, being active reduces your brain's excess *adrenaline*, the hormone that activates fight-or-flight responses.

Social connection. You can combine the mental health benefits of physical activity and social connection if you take an exercise class or have a workout buddy. But regardless of whether you choose to incorporate movement in social ways, be sure to intentionally cultivate opportunities to connect with others. While trauma too often damages your confidence in trusting people, we nevertheless all need others. Isolation deepens depression.

Nutrition and nourishment. It's important to nourish yourself with healthy foods, neither restricting consumption to self-punish or shrink, nor using food to push down or comfort painful memories. Feed yourself with loving care, including a balance of complex carbohydrates, proteins, and fruits and vegetables. Remember that your brain, including the *limbic system* emotion center and *HPA* hormone region, is a physical organ and will operate best when it's well nourished with the ingredients it needs to produce happiness hormones.

Sleep. This is an essential component of brain health. Research from the National Sleep Foundation reveals that only 20 percent of American adolescents sleep enough. Sleeping less than 8 to 10 hours puts you at a disadvantage in your quest for resilience and improved mental health. Prioritize giving yourself a gentle wind-down routine at night, setting your phone to "do not disturb," and getting in bed *at least* 9 hours before your morning alarm. Bedtime can be an excellent time to do simple meditation, visualization, gratitude practice, and deep breathing.

Joy. To these basic ingredients of movement, social connection, nutrition, and sleep, be sure to add the spice. Make time for the things that feed your spirit and soul, which make you feel alive and bring you joy.

If this sounds like a complete lifestyle overhaul, choose just one area in which to get started. As that becomes consistent, add one more. Keep moving forward as you fight for your own well-being. Give yourself grace when you are inconsistent or things don't go as planned. Every day is a good day to start fresh. It's about progress, not perfection. You are doing this, not to get it right for some external validation, but to show kindness and honor to yourself. And you are so worthy—never give up!

ANI'S STORY

Ani was curious when she saw yoga as one of the options for PE class at school. At first, she felt self-conscious. She was constantly comparing herself to her classmates. But slowly, week by week, she began to internalize the guidance of focusing on her own progress and keeping her awareness within her own space. She was used to hiding and disconnecting from her body, but in yoga she began to feel connected to, and trusting of, her bodily sensations.

She realized she had been holding her breath a lot, and as she learned to inhale and exhale with every movement, she noticed that she began finding strength and calm through her breath outside class, too. Sometimes certain movements made her feel vulnerable and reminded her of past trauma, but the teacher encouraged the class to listen to their bodies and not do anything that felt uncomfortable. Ani began to truly understand that she had choice and control.

As the weeks went on, Ani noticed her strength emerging and realized it was both physical and emotional. She'd never thought of herself as strong before. It was a revelation.

Her favorite part was the end of class when they'd lay on their mats to rest in *savasana*. The instructor suggested giving thanks in this quiet space for what their bodies were able to do for them that day. It was a revolutionary thought: instead of hating or berating her body, Ani could simply appreciate it as a resource—both in class and in the rest of life.

I Have a Question . . .

I know that getting enough sleep is important self-care, and I try, but I just can't fall asleep! My mind keeps going back to bad memories or stress from the day. How can I turn it off so I can rest?

This was a struggle for a long time for me, too. You've read about some general strategies in this workbook for relaxation and preparing yourself for sleep, but sometimes your ruminating thoughts just won't turn off. When that happens, try this:

Pick a random word with about six or seven letters that don't repeat. For example, "radish." Picture that word in your mind. Then go through the letters of the word one at a time, thinking of as many nouns as you can that begin with that letter. Using our example, you might think *rose, rhinoceros, rice, raspberry, ring, receipt, rainbow* . . . As you think of each noun, stop and picture that object or person in your mind. Really take time to form the image before going to the next word. After you've run out of "r" words, move on to the next letter. *Artichoke, antelope, aardvark, apple, algebra* . . .

This image-flipping technique engages the creative, imagery-producing *visual cortex* of your brain involved in producing dreams. By moving from one image to the next, you don't linger in the analytical part of your brain too long. You may find that you don't make it to the end of your word before you fall asleep.

Practice: Daily Mindfulness

Mindfulness can ground you and enhance your sense of well-being at any time of day. One powerful way to pause and practice mindfulness is through a morning intention-setting practice.

Upon waking, sit up in bed, resting your palms on your knees. (This is important so that you don't fall back asleep on those too early school mornings.) Close your eyes lightly and take some slow, deep breaths, filling your lungs completely, gently bringing vitality back into your body.

Allowing your mind to roam over the day ahead, consider what you most need. Focus? Energy? Patience? Courage? Peace? Then set your intention for the day, speaking it quietly aloud: *"Today, I will give myself grace." "I carry courage with me into school today." "Today I will practice patience." "I remain grounded and give myself peace through my breath today."*

Take a final deep, settling breath to seal your intention, then open your eyes. Stretch your arms out wide to the sides and high overhead, then rise to begin your day. Check in with yourself throughout the day, graciously reminding yourself of your intention as needed.

The beauty of an intention is that while it does increase your success at these goals, it is not a rigid pass-or-fail test. When you notice yourself getting away from the goal, gently refresh your intention with kindness and grace.

Multiple Choice: Gratitude Focus

For a lighthearted exploration of the many things in life for which you might be grateful, try this twist on "would you rather" questions. Select the item from each grouping that you are *most* grateful for in this moment. If it's hard to choose, recognize that's a good thing! You may find there is more goodness around than you realized.

I'm thankful for . . .

A. the smell of coffee
B. the taste of strawberries
C. that someone
    invented chocolate

A. rainbows
B. flowers
C. sunsets

A. my sense of vision
B. my sense of hearing
C. my sense of taste

A. oceans
B. lakes
C. rivers

A. modern medicine
B. modern plumbing
C. modern transportation

A. literacy
B. sports
C. art

A. having teeth
B. having fingernails
C. having hair

A. a friend
B. a family member
C. a teacher

A. video games
B. social media
C. movies

A. cats
B. dogs
C. horses

A. deodorant
B. toilet paper
C. hand sanitizer

A. rain
B. sunshine
C. snow

A. pillows
B. blankets
C. stuffed animals

A. spell-check
B. autosave
C. being able to look up
    anything online

A. when I don't have homework
B. going out
C. sleeping in

A. diversity
B. freedom
C. opportunity

Calendar: Daily Positive Moments

Creating new thinking and behavior patterns takes practice and consistency. As you put new mental health reinforcements into play, track your successes in the calendar that follows. Note any positive steps you took, new realizations or self-discoveries, or moments for which you are grateful. This calendar is to record and celebrate your successes.

SUNDAY	MONDAY	TUESDAY
ex: Went for a jog	Passed my test!	Got enough sleep

WEDNESDAY	THURSDAY	FRIDAY	SATURDAY
Played with my dog	*Saw my therapist*	*Sleepover with BFF!*	*Practiced meditation*

Writing Your Personal Affirmations

A personal affirmation is a short, positive statement that gently counters negative thought traps. Personal affirmations have the power to set your focus and intention, guiding you from negative thinking into an expansive space with room for hope and growth. They are tools to affirm or remind yourself of simple yet powerful and important truths. Throughout this book, you've found affirmations highlighted at the end of each chapter to guide you on your recovery path. As you move into post-traumatic growth work, you can learn to create your own, customized affirmations, or mantras, to use in your daily life.

AFFIRMATION BENEFITS

Affirmations can become mantras of self-encouragement. You can use them by repeating these phrases in times of challenge as well as in neutral times, such as the beginning of a new day. As you speak the words, listen to their truth and set your intention to live them out in the present. It can be helpful to close your eyes, lay a hand over your heart (or anywhere you feel anxiety), repeat the words, and pause, letting your mind linger as the truth of the words and intention settle into your mind and heart.

Research shows that using positive affirmations decreases stress, rumination (when your negative thoughts loop over and over), and the negative health impacts of stress. It can also increase success with goals, such as academics and implementing healthy habits, and improve your problem-solving capability. Together, these factors build your resilience.

Positive affirmations are also a part of the powerful trauma therapy approach, EMDR, that you read about in previous chapters. Developing positive self-beliefs, or positive cognitions as they're referred to in EMDR treatment, can create a foundation for effective reprocessing of your trauma and the work of replacing sticky negative beliefs. Or, if your positive belief came to you through EMDR work, daily meditation on this affirmation as a mantra can reinforce its power as you move forward and work to continue caring for your long-term mental health.

HOW TO START

Affirmations must be congruent with your own deeply held values to be useful and effective. If there's no element of truth or value in it, you'll never believe it, nor will you be encouraged by its repetition. Use your strengths as well as strengths you'd like to develop to guide the creation of your affirmations.

As you consider the words you need, think of where you're stuck. Perhaps there is a negative belief that is anchoring you to anxiety or depression. If you could rid yourself of these negative thoughts, what would you believe? Remaining connected to what is believable to you, rewrite that negative script using only positive words. For example, if you often think "I'm the worst," you don't have to meditate on "I'm the best" because unless you believe it just a little, it won't be helpful. Better to hold on to "I accept myself as I am" or "I am growing and becoming." You don't have to believe 100 percent in this affirmation yet, but it should at least have a seed of truth in it that can grow.

Affirmations don't have to be long. A few brief, carefully chosen words can be powerful, effective, and easier to remember. Avoid negatives, such as "I'm not _____." Swearing is okay though if it gives you a sense of power or reinforcement. Your own affirmations don't have to belong on a greeting card.

Write your affirmations in the first person (using *I* or *my*) and in the present tense rather than past or future. "I am becoming stronger each day" is more powerful than "I will be strong one day" or "I'm not scared anymore." Affirm what is, not what you need or feel you lack.

Practice your affirmations daily, when you get up, at natural transitions in your day, before big or challenging events, and as you lay down to rest. Breathe while repeating your affirmations, bringing calm and stillness into your mind and body. Believe the good in yourself, and watch it flourish!

Try out the following affirmations by speaking them aloud and considering how each resonates in your body and spirit. Then use the space provided in each topical section to write some affirmations of your own.

Affirmations for Personal Growth

I am growing and becoming.
I have choices and power.
I believe in who I am becoming.
I am whole just as I am.
I am worthy, whole, and complete.

_____ .

_____ .

_____ .

_____ .

_____ .

Affirmations for Daily Inspiration

There is beauty all around me.
Goodness and justice are always unfolding.
The universe is full of mystery and miracle, and I am a part of it.
I'm right where I need to be today.
I've got this.

_____.

_____.

_____.

_____.

_____.

Affirmations for Healing

I allow my heart to heal.
I am strong.
I embrace growth.
I am an overcomer.
I am brave enough to feel and strong enough to heal.

_____.

_____.

_____.

_____.

_____.

Affirmations for Your Relationships

I open my heart to love.
I can trust.
I choose honesty and openness.
I can speak up for myself.
I receive love and kindness.

_____.

_____.

_____.

_____.

_____.

Affirmations for Your Future

I embrace today as I build a bright tomorrow.
I create success day by day.
I have limitless potential.
My future has unlimited possibility.
I am full of hope.

_____ .

_____ .

_____ .

_____ .

_____ .

I am brave, strong, and resilient. I believe in myself.

Key Takeaways

- Resilience is your ability to adapt and overcome in times of crisis or struggle.

- Post-traumatic growth comes from making meaning and developing new inner resources as you heal from trauma.

- Resilience is built on self-compassion, interpersonal connections, purpose, consistency with self-care, and a habit of gratitude.

- A solid wellness routine involves physical activity, nutrition, sufficient sleep, social connection, and finding meaning in your life and purpose in the world.

- Writing and repeating daily positive affirmations decreases stress, counters self-limiting beliefs, and supports well-being and growth.

- Speaking positive truths aloud with loving-kindness can unleash your potential for post-traumatic growth.

CHAPTER 5

NAVIGATING YOUR SOCIAL WORLD

Social life can be challenging after trauma. Many people feel different or ashamed, like they can't relate to others or are afraid that someone might figure out their buried secrets. For others, the depression or anxiety that comes from trauma leads to withdrawing into a safe, protective shell. It can be scary to contemplate sharing your story for fear of rejection or of overwhelming others, yet the sense of isolation when your truth is hidden can be painful.

The effects of trauma are revealed in different ways in relationships as patterns of fight, flight, freeze, fawn, flock, or fade are played out. You might unintentionally harm relationships when triggered to a *fight* reaction or run away in a *flight* response to tension, leaving conflicts unresolved. You might *freeze* and find yourself feeling disconnected, dissociated, out of body, and unable to find words to connect with those around you. If you've suffered relational trauma, you might *fawn* or become whatever the other person wants in order to keep them happy. You might immerse yourself in a caregiving role in a *flock* pattern to prove your worth or *fade* away from others in avoidance.

Consider how your trauma impacts your social world so that you can take conscious steps to minimize negative effects and foster the sort of relationships you desire, and that support you. Human connection is essential and, when healthy, incredibly rewarding. Let's look at how you can reengage your social world in healthy ways.

Evaluating Your Relationships

Crisis can bring out the best and worst in people. When you go through a traumatic event, you may find the people around you reveal themselves in new ways. You may be surprised by who shows up for you and who is incapable of holding space.

You may also find that your own values, priorities, and interests shift because of your experience, causing you to draw closer to certain people and drift from others. Such a crucible may sharpen your awareness of what you want and need in the people closest to you. No one person is likely to be or provide all that you need, and that's okay. Enjoy the relationship for what it is as long as it's not harmful. Surround yourself with a variety of people you enjoy in different ways. But also know that it's okay—even good—to let go of toxic, unhealthy, unenjoyable, or unhelpful relationships. Just be sure to balance that pruning process by cultivating new connections or nurturing other existing relationships.

In healthy relationships you feel seen, heard, and supported. You should be able to be your full, true self without having to edit parts or prove yourself. You can have fun and be silly but also show sad or other difficult emotions. Healthy relationships bring out the best in you, and you like and can be proud of who you are when you are with them. Most importantly, there should be a sense of equality between you. Not every relationship will have this level of depth, and relationships play different roles, but never settle for relationships in which you are expected to change who you are to be accepted.

WHAT DO YOU NEED?

In addition to these broad principles of equality and acceptance, consider what you personally need in your relationships. This may differ across relationship types, such as adults, friends, and perhaps dating if that is something you are exploring at this time. (It's totally okay if you are not interested in dating, too. While some date during their teen years, many well-adjusted people begin dating after high school, and some are not interested in romance or sexuality at all. There's no right or wrong answer here.)

Perhaps you feel a need for safety, security, and protection in those you live with. You might crave a friend with whom you can just be silly and have fun, or a close confidant to whom you can tell your secrets and struggles. Perhaps you long for a mentor figure or surrogate parent type to fill a void in your life. You might desire friends who will be allies in a newfound passion or cause, such as combating climate change, advocating for gun control, stopping drunk driving, finding a cure for pediatric cancer, or fighting rape culture as your experience exposed you to societal vulnerabilities. Maybe there are behaviors that you once accepted as normal in relationships, but that are no longer tolerable to you.

Spend some time in reflection to identify what you truly need and want. This can help you move toward relationships with intentionality versus reactivity and decrease any propensity to spend time with people who pull you down the wrong path.

TAKING STOCK

As you consider what you need and desire in your social support circle, take time to evaluate the relationships already present in your life. Think of your friends, dates, family members (those you live with, whether related to you or not, and extended family), classmates, teachers, teammates, religious community members and leaders, managers, and coworkers. Who has shown themselves to be genuine, reliable, and true? Who can you trust to be who they say they are and follow through when you need them? With whom do you feel comfortable and confident, and who makes you feel self-conscious and awkward? Do you feel small, dirty, bad, or ashamed when you are with certain people? With whom are you the best version of yourself?

Have any of these relationships changed with time or in response to the trauma? While some traumas happen in secrecy, causing you to feel alone with your pain from the beginning, others impact you along with your community, which creates unique challenges in your relationships. If that is your experience, you may find yourself feeling closer than ever to those with whom you went through the trauma. At the same time, many collective trauma survivors are afraid to talk with fellow survivors for fear of triggering their peers and suffer isolation as a result. You may also find that non-survivor family and friends tiptoe around you in fear of doing the same to you, leaving you feeling alone when you just want to be treated normally. You may feel excluded from the inner circle if you were less directly impacted by the event, as happens too often to survivors of school shootings who were in a different classroom, or who were present but physically unharmed. Isolation after trauma is common, and it is painful.

Sometimes trauma happens within the context of relationship, leaving deep *attachment* wounds and injury to your ability to trust. Experiencing an assault from a date, abuse from a relative or parent, or betrayal from a friend all reveal toxicity where you may not have previously perceived it. Know you have the right and the power to set limits and leave such unhealthy relationships. Although the leaving may result in a sense of emptiness at first, you will not always be alone. Not everyone will treat you so callously. Your heart can heal and love again.

HEALING STRATEGIES

Though there are many advantages to addressing trauma while still a teenager, there is one distinct disadvantage: You have limited control over your life circumstances. You may be living within an abusive dynamic or be placed in repeated contact with someone who has harmed you. You don't always have a choice regarding the people you live with.

While these circumstances are truly difficult, you are not without power. If you live in an unsafe home, talk to a trusted teacher about it. There may be options to live with a friend or cousin. These things are hard and scary, and the status quo feels safer even when it is fundamentally unsafe. I know. But do not dismiss the truth that you deserve safety. Call a youth help hotline (there are several listed in the Resources section on page 164) or reach out for help from a trusted adult right away.

This same sense of powerlessness easily pervades other relationships, including unhealthy friendships and dating connections. You *do* have power though! You have options. Your wants and wishes matter.

Leave toxic romances. Love respects and does not harm.

Tell someone. If you are being manipulated or threatened, talk to someone who can help you sort out what to do. Do not expect that the person causing you harm will change or fool yourself into thinking you can fix them by putting up with abuse for the sake of love or loyalty.

Set limits and boundaries. This important skill can help you reshape unhealthy relationships.

Change classes or schools. If you are being bullied at school, press your parents, teachers, or school counselor to switch classes or schools. You deserve safety.

Advocate for your needs. Even in average relationships, be your own best friend by speaking up when you are hurting or in need. For example, you might ask your family not to treat you like you are fragile because of what you went through, or you might have a conversation about your triggers, requesting extra sensitivity around certain sensory cues.

Repeat positive affirmations. When you struggle to speak up for yourself, use affirmations to remind yourself of your worth and to set your intention for what you desire in your social sphere. Affirmations can also strengthen you when you want to share your story with a proven and trusted friend but feel afraid.

Explore and acknowledge your fears. Take the time to identify limiting beliefs that hold you back.

Craft positive replacement thoughts. These can help you set an intention moving forward.

You are not damaged goods. You are not shameful. You are lovable and worthy of love.

RAE'S STORY

Rae had been happy at her new school until one day when Josh transferred there, too. He stared at her throughout first period, making her squirm. When the bell rang, he approached her, blocking her exit from the classroom as the other students waited behind them. "I know you," Josh said with a smirk. "You're Raymond."

Rae's face turned white as she watched her classmates process her deadname. "Wait. I thought Rae was short for Rachel," a student behind Josh said. Everything changed from that day forward. Teasing turned to bullying and culminated one awful day when she was shoved into the boys' restroom and locked inside.

Rae stuck to herself after that, keeping her head down and ignoring the taunts as best she could. So, when Leah asked to be her lab partner, Rae was suspicious. But slowly she began to accept Leah's gestures of friendship. As she cautiously opened up, Rae began to rewrite her internal stories about her own worthiness. Without noticing, she began to hold her head higher and look others in the eye.

When a new student joined the class and Josh coughed out the name "Raymond" as she was introducing herself, Rae lifted her chin and confidently asserted, "Just *Rae*. And my pronouns are *she/her*."

I Have a Question . . .

My parents finally separated after I'd spent years watching my dad beat up my mom. I have nightmares from those days. But the judge is making me visit my dad every week. I don't have any respect for him, and I don't want to go. Is there anything I can do?

It's so unfair when youth are forced into situations that are unwanted and feel unsafe. I encourage you to advocate for yourself at every opportunity, both by attending court hearings and asking to speak, and by verbalizing your concerns to both parents. If it feels safe, be direct in telling your father you'd rather not come. Consider consulting with a psychologist who might be able to advocate on your behalf in court regarding the impact of such visits.

Change what you can, and focus your energy where you have control. When there is nothing more you can do to limit the unwanted contact, turn your energy to managing the time in ways that will most support your mental health. It could help to fill that time by catching up on homework, practicing music lessons, or calling a friend. Then you can enjoy your free time with the parent with whom you feel more comfortable.

Push to have visits in public spaces where your dad may be more self-controlled. Journal during or after a visit about what happens and how it makes you feel, both to create a record and to have a therapeutic outlet. Keep your phone charged and have an emergency plan if he should become volatile. Plan post-visit self-care strategies to soothe the triggered stress such visits cause. Finally, be conscious of any negative thoughts or critical self-talk that creep in during your time with your father, compassionately providing self-reassurance and encouragement.

Know that this will end—it won't last forever. Keep lifting your voice until it is heard.

Quiz: Healthy Relationships

Take this quick true/false quiz to assess the health of a relationship about which you are having doubts or experiencing stress. If you get mostly *false* answers, it may be time to begin setting boundaries and withdrawing from this relationship as you build up alternatives. If you answer each question with a T for *true*, lean in! If it's something in between, keep your eyes open and move forward cautiously.

T / F   I feel physically safe with this person.

T / F   I feel emotionally safe with this person.

T / F   I'm not afraid to ask for what I want.

T / F   I can say "no" when I don't want something.

T / F   I can say "stop" and they will stop.

T / F   I can be myself.

T / F   I share my secrets with them.

T / F   I feel respected and liked.

T / F   We treat each other as equals.

T / F   We have fun together.

Fill in the Blanks: Evaluating My Relationships

Who are the solid rocks in your social support circle? Use the following exercise to reflect on any healthy relationships in your life, whether adult or peer. You might repeat some names or identify several people. Those about whom you can readily fill in these blanks are ones to treasure, and perhaps allow yourself to open up with even more.

I like being with _____ because _____.

They help me when _____.

I trust them because _____.

Someone I can talk to when I'm upset is _____.

I feel safe with them because _____.

I always have a good time with _____.

We have fun together doing _____.

_____ is someone I know I can turn to when I need help.

I feel good about myself when I am with _____.

They show me respect when _____.

I can tell _____ anything, and I know they will accept me.

Table: My Support System

Who comprises your support system? If you feel as though you don't have one, who is in your life who might support you, with whom you could work on building or strengthening a relationship? Consider the categories in the chart that follows. It's okay if some categories remain blank. Even so, as you consider the multiple realms of your life, you may find there is more loving support surrounding you than you knew.

	NAME(S)	HOW THEY SUPPORT ME OR SIGNS THEY MIGHT BE A SUPPORTIVE PERSON
Family—immediate		
Family—extended relatives		
Friends		
Dating		
Teachers and school personnel		
Religious leaders		
Coaches		
Others (therapist, social worker, mentor)		

Practicing Healthy Communication

Good communication is foundational to healthy relationships. Relationships after trauma are no exception. It can be challenging to navigate the uncertain terrain of triggers within and around your social world, and what is not expressly stated can be too easily misunderstood and taken personally. As you find words to communicate your needs, tell your story, and express your boundaries, you grow in your sense of inner power and strength. Finding others willing to listen, respect, and receive your communication melts isolation along with negative beliefs about your worth and ability to trust, and reinforces your positive affirmations.

TWO-WAY COMMUNICATION

Communication consists of two parts: listening and speaking. We often focus more on expressive skills than receptive skills, but one without the other is useless.

Listening is more than being quiet while someone else talks. It is not simply waiting for your turn while planning a response or argument to the first thing you heard; rather, it is crucial to listen for the fullness of what the other person is trying to communicate. Listening is an active process wherein you hold an intention to understand not only the words being said but also the feelings, fears, and hopes behind them. This is unlikely to happen immediately or automatically, and usually requires you to ask clarifying questions or invite more information. You might also summarize what you hear in your own words to be sure you understand the intention. In addition to trying to fully understand, an important listening skill is communicating your receptive posture through an open stance, expressions of interest and empathy, and even micro-verbalizations such as "mm-hm," "oh wow," "mmm . . .," "yikes," or whatever language is natural between you.

As you communicate your receptivity to hearing what the other is sharing, moving from open body language to micro-expressions to clarifying or summarizing questions, you should have an opportunity to share your reactions, thoughts, feelings, and needs, as well. You might also be the one to open a dialogue, and these same principles apply. Healthy communication comes from your authentic self. Take time to clarify internally what you feel, need, or want, both for yourself and for the other person. For big topics, it can even be helpful to journal and organize your thoughts on paper before approaching the other person.

Speak for yourself assertively using "I" language. For example, it is more effective to express "I feel really anxious when I don't hear from you for hours. Could you just respond with 'I can't talk now' so I know we're okay?" It's easy to simply level an accusation: "You never respond to my texts." However, this approach tends to cause conflicts that don't achieve what you truly want.

Effective and healthy communication is direct, not channeling your wishes or frustrations through a third person. It involves some vulnerability as you speak for yourself and are honest about your feelings. Good communicators consider the timing of important conversations, approaching when neither person is likely to be overtired, stressed, or distracted by something else, or have limited time. It is considerate and helpful to ask, "Do you have the time and emotional space to talk right now?" before unloading a heavy topic. Don't assume that because they may not be available that they don't care and won't want to listen another time. Your words matter, and true friends and safe people will want to be there for you.

HEALING STRATEGIES

The critical challenge in healing from trauma is reestablishing a sense of safety. This is true on an internal, or sensory, level; a physical, or environmental, level; as well as a social and emotional level.

Words are powerful. Perhaps you've felt stripped of power in what you went through. As you use your voice to speak your truth and express your needs, you may begin to feel your power return. It can be difficult to break through fears that kept you silent, yet it can be healing when you speak and find others don't run away. You may feel helpless against being mistreated, but every time you set a boundary and speak assertively, you reinforce the truths that your needs matter and you do have power. Each time you speak up, you melt a bit of the trauma *freeze* with the warm breath of your voice.

To thaw the social freeze:

Reflect. Take some time to consider not only what you'd like to communicate but also the fears holding you back. Are there self-limiting beliefs, negative self-conceptions you took on through your trauma that constrain you? Notice what's underneath, and regard those fears with tender compassion.

Speak truth and affirmation to your fearful parts. Perhaps enlist the help of a trauma therapist if you can't find a way around it.

Take courage. The risk will be worth the reward when you find that you don't have to carry your burdens alone, don't have to remain locked in isolation, don't have to always feel different or unlovable. You are enough, and you are not too much.

I Have a Question . . .

I've been dating a great guy for a couple of months now, but sometimes he does things that make me have flashbacks and freeze. I think I need to tell him what happened to me, but I'm so scared he'll be disgusted and dump me. I don't know what to say or do!

It sounds like you feel really torn, your secret bursting to be set free while you remain terrified to let it out. The scariest part of telling our stories to new people is the question of how they'll react and how it might change the relationship dynamic. I can't promise you the outcome you desire. I do suspect though that you'll be better off on the other side of the telling. Because if he can't handle your truth, he isn't worthy of you, and the sooner you know this, the less painful the separation will be. But if he is the great guy that you believe him to be (and there's no sign he's prone to gossip), he'll show empathy and support, and your relationship will grow and deepen as a result. You'll have an easier time expressing your boundaries, and he'll understand them more fully, too.

Consider carefully what you'd like to say, writing it out and practicing it aloud in privacy. Keep it simple; he doesn't need all the details. Then when you're ready, set it up by asking if it's a good time to share something with him, so you have his full attention and are respectful of his emotional capacity. No matter how it goes, know that his reaction does *not* indicate who you are, your value, or your goodness. These things are innate and intrinsic to you, and no one's opinion can move them.

Test: Communication Strengths and Weaknesses

How strong are your communication skills? Take the following test to assess where you are. Circle the number in the column for *never, sometimes, often,* or *always* to respond to each question, then add up the numbers you've circled to get your score. The closer your score is to 35, the better your communication. Take a look at where you score low to get a better understanding of areas to work on, then come back in a few months and take the test again.

	NEVER	SOMETIMES	OFTEN	ALWAYS
The best time to talk is whenever something is on my mind.	1	3	2	0
I check to make sure the other person has the emotional space to talk before I begin.	0	1	2	3
The best topic is me.	1	2	1	0
I make jokes to avoid discomfort.	3	2	1	0
I try to understand why the other person is saying what they are saying.	0	1	2	3
I interject as soon as I know where they are going.	3	2	1	0
I cross my arms, look away, check my phone, or roll my eyes until they are done talking.	3	2	1	0
I show I am listening by nodding, smiling, or looking concerned as appropriate.	0	1	2	3
I start by expressing my feelings using "I" language.	0	1	2	3
I express what I want as a request rather than a criticism.	0	1	2	3
It's important that I make the other person understand they messed up.	2	3	1	0
If it can't get worked out in one conversation, it's not worth it.	2	3	1	0

Checklist: Active Listening

Life presents many opportunities to practice the skills of becoming an active listener. The next time someone is telling you something, whether they are calm or upset, try following this checklist and see how it changes the dynamic.

☐ Keep an open posture (leaning in, arms uncrossed).

☐ Make eye contact and observe the speaker's body language.

☐ Show empathic facial expressions and body language.

☐ Give micro-verbalizations of understanding and empathy (*mm, oh wow, yikes, okay,* etc.).

☐ Invite more information.

☐ Ask clarifying questions.

☐ Summarize to check understanding.

☐ Share reactions and respond.

Outline for Assertive Communication

When you want to communicate something difficult, it can help to have a plan. You might outline what you want to say and even practice it out loud in your bedroom or in front of the bathroom mirror. Consider the following pieces of assertive communication as you craft your approach. This can be especially helpful in talking with parents.

- Timing
  - When will they be most receptive and least distracted, tired, or busy?
  - When are you feeling most rested and confident?
  - When is the best time to talk that will allow enough time for the whole conversation?
- Define the issue: It helps to keep the conversation on one issue without pulling in past problems or future worries.
- Review what is known about the topic.
- Identify your feelings about the topic.
- Express your wants:
  - For yourself
  - For the other person
  - For anyone else affected
- Make your request.
- Consider their feedback. Use your active listening skills.
- Set a time to return to the topic if:
  - More information needs to be gathered.
  - Time is needed to reflect on the conversation or make decisions.
  - You agreed to try a specific solution for a time and need to reassess.
- Thank them for their time, for listening, and for considering your feelings and position.

Setting Boundaries

A boundary is a limit communicated verbally and reinforced with action that serves to protect your physical or emotional space.

Boundaries protect and empower you. They allow you to create the space you need to feel safe, relaxed, and comfortable. Setting clear boundaries is kind to those around you because you don't leave others guessing what you want or need. Most importantly, communicating your boundaries is an act of self-care.

When you are consistent in setting and reinforcing healthy boundaries, you can let people in with less fear of being controlled or overwhelmed by them. This gives you more freedom to explore relationships and develop the social support that you need. At the same time, you experience increased independence by firmly limiting others' ability to control or run your life. Boundaries allow you to accept the help you need, or could use, without fear of losing autonomy.

Enacting boundaries also protects your mental health. You can decide how much of others' problems you are willing to shoulder, finding the space that feels right between being helpful and taking responsibility for what is not yours to carry. Finding this healthy limit allows you to focus on your own healing while remaining a caring friend. Such boundaries empower you to be the involved person you desire for the long term while avoiding over-responsibility that leads to burnout.

WHERE TO START?

Begin with self-reflection and an honest self-assessment of your emotional capacity. This can fluctuate from day to day or from week to week, or based on your current life stage and responsibilities. Therefore, some boundaries may be flexible in response to ever-changing personal needs and availability while others remain firm. Flexible boundaries do not mean a lack of boundaries.

Boundaries are internally constructed and externally communicated. You may develop an internal standard that says, "I do not spend time with this person when I am feeling exhausted." You would then communicate your boundary externally by expressing your unavailability rather than feeling helpless to control the expenditure of your time, energy, and needs.

Negotiating boundaries requires balancing responsibilities to others and yourself. No matter how old you are, there are some things that will tap into your physical and psychological energy that are nonnegotiable facts of life. This may include responsibilities to family, pets, and school. Nevertheless, you are not required to submit to abuse in any domain. You may need to find ways to set limits within fulfillment of obligations, such as standing up for yourself when spoken to disrespectfully.

The most significant universal task of adolescence is navigating the transition from dependence to independence. Following trauma, this typically rocky road can be even more difficult as parents may protectively pull you close while you feel the natural inner pull toward independence, or you may feel a need for greater protection and fear the developmental stages of increasing separation. Communicating your feelings and needs clearly will decrease the tension and stress as you respectfully but firmly set boundaries within the contexts of family and other responsibilities.

HEALING STRATEGIES

When you've experienced trauma, it can be challenging to set boundaries. It's easy to doubt that your needs matter when others have treated you as though they don't. You might be afraid to speak up if this has led to violence in the past. You might freeze in fear and find that no words escape your lips. Or perhaps the constant feeling of being on edge leaves you prone to anger. To avoid fights, you say nothing until you become overwhelmed.

Despite these challenges, boundary setting is a skill that, like any other skill, can be learned and strengthened with practice.

Remind yourself that boundaries are good. It is not selfish or mean to say no. It is not your job to ensure that other people are happy. You deserve the protection your boundaries can provide.

Identify your needs. What do you need more or less of to feel comfortable or safe? Do your aunt's constant questions about the fire overwhelm you? Does your dad's fast driving trigger flashbacks of the accident? Is your boyfriend moving too fast?

Express what you need. Once you've identified what you want changed, play around with wording to figure out how you might communicate it. You can use the fill-in-the-blanks exercise on page 123 to get started. A strong, assertive message often begins with "I need" and clearly identifies what action the other person should change.

Back up your boundaries with action. You might say, "Taylor, I feel weird when you touch me like that. Please don't." If Taylor doesn't respect your request, you can back up the boundary by getting up, moving away, or even going home.

When you're ready to speak your needs, take a deep breath. Acknowledge your fears with self-compassion. Then lift your chin as you tap into your inner courage. You've got this.

Remember: you matter, your needs matter, and your boundaries are good.

LEO'S STORY

Learning to navigate the world with his new prosthetic was a frightening yet exciting challenge for Leo. Months on crutches since the accident took his foot had left him feeling helpless and angry. He hated needing help for so many things.

The prosthetic couldn't erase what had happened, but leaving the crutches behind felt like a big step in reclaiming his independence. Unfortunately, his worried mother continued to hover, jumping up to bring him things before he could get up and doing tasks he used to do. While it might once have been nice to avoid chores, now it just reinforced his sense of being broken.

"Mom," Leo said, "I really appreciate how much you care and want to help. But I need to do things for myself again. I promise I will ask for help when I need it. But I need you to let me try first."

Leo's mom expressed understanding, but she sometimes forgot. So, Leo backed up his boundary with action. When she grabbed his plate after dinner before he could stand up, Leo purposely cleared his sister's plate and the serving dish. It felt good to exercise his independence and build his strength. As she saw Leo demonstrate his competence, his mom began to relax, too.

Quiz: Identifying My Boundaries

Consider how you might respond in the following scenarios. Which seem like the best responses? What alternatives can you think of on your own? Which responses are you most likely to use?

You're exhausted from a week of school, band practice, and babysitting your brother. Your friend asks you to sleep over Friday night. Do you:

A. *Say yes because you don't want to hurt their feelings?*

B. *Say "No, thanks"?*

C. *Suggest an alternate night?*

Your boyfriend slips his hand under your clothes while you're kissing, and you don't like it. Do you:

A. *Grab his hand and move it away?*

B. *Just go with it—he paid for dinner, so you owe him?*

C. *Tell him "I'm not ready for that," and get up if he tries again?*

Your friend is telling you the juicy gossip they heard about your other friend. Do you:

A. *Figure there's no harm in listening as long as you're not spreading it to anyone else?*

B. *Ask for more details?*

C. *Tell them you're not comfortable talking about the other person when they're not present?*

Your older brother tells you he's planning a party while your parents are away. He says you can join in if you don't tell. Do you:

A. Plan your outfit?

B. Tell your parents they might want to ask your brother about his plans while they're gone?

C. Arrange to sleep over at a friend's house that night?

The students sitting with you in the cafeteria start making racist jokes. Do you:

A. Laugh uncomfortably?

B. Tell a staff person?

C. Say "that's not actually funny," and move to a new seat if they continue?

Your uncle always looks at you a little too long and makes comments about your outfits at family gatherings. Do you:

A. Start wearing large, baggy clothes whenever he's around?

B. Tell him "I'd rather you didn't comment on my appearance," and walk away to be with your cousin?

C. Politely ignore him?

Fill in the Blanks: Establishing My Boundaries

Let's practice creating boundaries with some fill-in-the-blank sentences. You can customize these to your needs, wants, and comfort level. Then, practice saying them out loud, perhaps in front of a mirror. When you're ready, pick the one that seems easiest and try it out.

I am not comfortable with _____.

If you continue to _____,

I will _____.

Example: I am not comfortable with those jokes. If you keep talking like that, I'm just going to head home.

I feel _____ when

we _____.

Let's do _____ instead.

Example: I feel anxious when we watch movies with shooting scenes. Let's watch a comedy instead.

When you _____, I feel _____.

Please _____.

That doesn't work for me. Why don't we _____

_____.

I don't do _____. Thanks for offering though!

I'm not ready for _____ yet.

Sorry, I can't _____

tonight. Maybe another time.

I need you to warn me before _____.

I'd rather not talk about _____.

I appreciate your concern though.

Table: My Boundaries for Different Relationships

Different relationships come with diverse challenges, and therefore require different boundaries to maintain both your psychological well-being and the health of the relationship. Consider the significant relationships in your life and use the following chart to note some boundaries that may be needed.

PERSON	PROBLEM	BOUNDARY NEEDED	WORDS TO SET BOUNDARY	ACTIONS TO REINFORCE BOUNDARY

Script: Talking about My Boundaries

Boundaries are as unique as you, your needs, comfort levels, circumstances, and relationships. Therefore, there's no solid script to memorize to fit every person and situation. However, there's a general formula you can apply to express and back up your limits with others. Consider the various challenges in your life and visualize using this formula to create the physical and psychological protections you desire.

When you _____,

I feel _____. I need

you to (stop/start/ask first) _____

when _____. If you do

not _____, I will

_____.

It is crucial that you do not make idle threats because you will undermine your own boundaries. Pick an action that you know you can follow through on and be sure to give yourself permission to do that thing if your boundary is violated. As you show yourself to be resolute and consistent, others should eventually come to respect your boundary.

Learning to Trust Again

Interpersonal trauma attacks not only your body but your ability to trust, too. Without healing, the experience of such a hurt continues to cause suffering throughout time. It can be hard to feel emotionally and perhaps physically safe with others again. This may be narrowed to certain categories of people, leading to biases and prejudices, or generalized to all people, leaving you in effect alone in a crowded world.

This places you in a double bind: afraid to trust, yet lonely. There looms before you an immense hurdle: do you risk all that you fear, whether judgment, shame, rejection, or abuse, plunging bravely through for the hope of healing connection, or remain safely wrapped in comfortable, if cold, solitude? Moving from this uncomfortable valley takes true courage. It may not be without psychological bruises, but ultimately the choice to let love in will set you free.

LETTING PEOPLE IN

Taking courage and risking hurt to open yourself to new and deeper relationships creates the possibility of heart-level healing. As you challenge your negative beliefs regarding yourself, others, and *trust* itself, you open the possibility for these beliefs to melt in the light of warm truth. Shame, the shadowy legacy of trauma, flourishes in secrecy and silence.

Do you believe you are unlovable? Gross? Too much? Not enough? Do you fear that no one would understand, or that others would distance themselves if they knew your secret? Such fears reinforce depression and anxiety. Protecting them allows their roots to grow. Exposing them will cause them to wither.

I can't promise that the first person you open your heart to will understand. I wish I could offer that reassurance. But as you carefully consider the signs of a trustworthy person, taking time to get to know your would-be confidant, the likelihood grows that they will embrace all of you and your story. And if the first person you tell can't hold your heart in the ways that you need, press on—there surely will be others who do. The reward of openhearted acceptance and a relationship of authenticity is worth the risk.

HEALING STRATEGIES

When trust has shattered and relationships feel threatening, it can help to start your outward expansion slowly, with safe reparative relationships. Therapy can provide this experience of a safe, trusting, accepting relationship that can be a template for future healthy relationships even while working toward your specific recovery goals. Additionally, in their own ways connections with animals can provide lower-stakes healing attachments as you experience the interactive bonding process.

As you move forward in developing healthy relationships, take some time to reflect, visualize, and plan.

Identify your negative beliefs about yourself and others. Then thoughtfully develop some replacement positive affirmations to meditate and reflect on. EMDR therapy can help you move away from feeling the negative is factual to believing the affirmation is true.

Learn the signs of trustworthy people and those who are unsafe. Choose friends and support systems consciously. Trust your own instincts and allow that trust to lead outward to trust of others.

- Trustworthy people are open and treat you and others with respect, kindness, and equality. They are honorable even when others aren't watching.

- Unsafe people lie, gossip, ask you to keep secrets, put others down, brag about themselves, are jealous, quick-tempered, controlling, and coercive, and demonstrate prejudice.

Visualize. As you take steps toward authenticity within existing relationships or make gestures to initiate new friendships, prepare yourself by visualizing a positive outcome and rehearsing what you might say. Decide what you want to disclose and what you want to hold on to for now. Rather than asking, "What's the worst that could happen," sit with the question of "What's the best that could happen?"

Set up a time to have a heart-to-heart with someone you already know. Be careful not to *trauma dump* and overwhelm a friend by suddenly off-loading a heavy story on someone without first checking to see if they are in a space for it.

Take deep breaths. Take your time and breathe slowly to calm and steady your nerves.

Believe in yourself. Approach others with confidence in the truth of your great worth!

I Have a Question . . .

I would love to work on deepening trust in relationships, but I don't have
any real friendships to work with. I don't know where to start!

I'm glad you want to work on building up this important aspect of your life. It suggests you realize at least to some degree that you have something good to offer and are worthy of love.

Start by reflecting on this truth. Your loneliness may have many causes, but none of them are inherent unworthiness. You are good and deserving of love and friendship.

Second, accept that you don't have to be everyone's cup of tea. Embrace your uniqueness and let go of the pressure to conform or to judge yourself against the social hierarchy. You'll know deepest happiness when you find those who really get you, and vice versa.

Then put yourself out there by engaging in the things that interest you. Are there after-school clubs, sports, activities, or groups that pique your interest? How can you use your unique talents or passions to connect with others? You might consider joining a service or activism group to help animals, the environment, or social justice causes. Perhaps there is a youth group at the synagogue, mosque, temple, or church you belong to with opportunities to get involved. If you play an instrument, consider joining a band or orchestra.

As you find ways to connect, take the final step of introducing yourself and initiating conversation. Show interest in the other person and try not to worry about how they perceive you. Others will be attracted to a caring, engaged, and confident you!

PRACTICE: TRUSTING
RELATIONSHIP VISUALIZATION

When taking the courageous step of putting yourself out there to make new relationship connections, it can help to put fears to rest by visualizing a positive outcome.

- Find a comfortable seat and rest your hands palms up on your knees in a posture of open reception. Gently close your eyes and deepen your breath. Breathe in slowly, visualizing inhaling love, belonging, acceptance, or friendship. Hold on to that for a beat, then slowly exhale, releasing fear, self-consciousness, apprehension, shame, or anything that holds you back. Continue this pattern for several minutes.

- Picture opening up a little bit more with someone who you know or taking some step to deepen the relationship. Visualize feeling safe, emotionally embraced, and supported by this person. Just sit with it as you continue to breathe. Remind yourself: *I can trust. I am loving and lovable.*

- When you are ready, place your hands palms down on your knees or as a seal over your heart. Take a last deep breath as you blink your eyes back open and rise to live out these truths.

Quiz: My Trust Level

Use the quiz below to assess your present level of trust. Rate the following questions as follows: **1**: Never, **2**: Seldom, **3**: Sometimes, **4**: Often, **5**: Always. Add up your score for Part 1 and for Part 2, then subtract your Part 1 score from your Part 2 score to get your Trust Level Score. As you continue to heal, come back to this tool again to see how you are growing.

PART 1	
I expect people will hurt me.	
I anticipate humiliation.	
Anything I say can and will be used against me.	
Everyone is out for themselves; it's a dog-eat-dog world.	
PART 2	
There are some people I can trust.	
Not every hurt or insult is intentional or personal.	
Others will be there for me when I need them.	
Some people are dependable.	
Some people keep their promises.	
Those I am close to care about my well-being.	
Those I am close to consider me when they make decisions.	
I can be my authentic self with those I love.	
I expect those close to me will keep my secrets.	
I expect the people close to me will be honest with me.	
I know that those close to me will respond kindly when I admit mistakes.	
I can be honest with others when I am upset about something.	

Fill in the Blanks: What Trust Means to Me

As you bravely open yourself to the possibilities of trust, take some time to reflect on what trust means to you personally. You can use the sentence prompts that follow to get started.

Trust is when I can _____.

Trust and _____ cannot coexist.

Trust feels _____.

I feel safe when _____.

To trust someone, I need _____.

I trust people who _____.

I cannot trust people who _____.

Trustworthy people _____.

There are _____ people I can trust.

I open my heart and share my truths with courage and confidence.

I am surrounded by love. I open my heart to let love flow in and out.

Key Takeaways

- Relationships may become strained after trauma due to fight, flight, freeze, fawn, flock, or fade reactions.

- Relationships are an essential component of healing and living a happy life.

- Take inventory of current relationships so you can reduce, remove, or replace unhealthy ones and build solid friendships and support systems.

- Strengthening your communication skills will improve your relationships. This involves both active listening and assertive communication.

- Boundaries protect your emotional and physical space and are important for every healthy relationship. Boundaries are expressed verbally and backed with action.

- As you heal from what happened, allow your heart to open and begin to trust again, looking for signs of safe people, so that you can enjoy the benefits of the warm relationships you deserve.

CHAPTER 6

EMBRACING YOUR FUTURE

Emerging from the darkness of what lies behind, there is so much light ahead. As you continue to do the work of recovery and reach toward post-traumatic growth, hopefully you have come to realize that the past is but a part of your story. It does not define you. With loving compassion for any hurt parts inside, allow your brave, adventurous, and curious parts to arise to create and embrace the beauty and possibilities that your precious life has to offer.

Reaching Acceptance

One of the greatest gifts you can give yourself on your path of healing is acceptance. This does not mean you redefine traumatic experiences as having been all right, but that you accept that they did happen and are a part of your life story. This allows you to integrate your experiences and leave behind wrestling with them in denial and anger. As you acknowledge what is, a quiet stillness can emerge, creating a place of calm from which you can build as you look ahead to construct the next story of your life.

Acceptance becomes possible as you build on the work you have already done. You have learned about trauma and created a framework for making sense of what happened. You have learned to understand, accept, and soothe your emotions, built awareness of harmful thought patterns, developed strategies for resilience, and begun to rebuild your social world. You've come so far! Allow yourself to celebrate your growth as a survivor and overcomer.

YOUR PAST DOESN'T DEFINE YOU

You are so much more than what happened to you. As you heal from and integrate that past, you might change and grow in new and beautiful ways. You can allow the past to be behind while becoming the you who you want to be, crystallizing the pain and lessons learned into a strong warrior self, with tender compassion, wisdom, and understanding. The hurt may have lit a fire in your belly that burns brightly in newfound passion for change. You might move through the world with a deeper sensitivity to the potential struggles of others. As you grow and become, the trauma may be the grain of sand in an oyster from which a lovely and precious pearl is formed.

And even as such beautiful truths are realized, the trauma does not define you. As the trauma is processed, it can be filed away, where you can retrieve it to look at when you want to, but where it no longer needs to consume your every thought, feeling, or reaction. You regain freedom to be fully in the present, to taste and smell and see in full color all the beauty and adventure life has to offer. You can become who you want to become and pursue what energizes you. The present and future are yours.

HEALING STRATEGIES

Self-acceptance comes as the culmination of all your healing work. As you meditate on the truth that you are not to blame, releasing yourself from self-criticism and shame, you gain a measure of distance and freedom from the pain of the past.

Self-acceptance grows as you get to know yourself beyond what happened to you.

- Affirm that what happened to you impacted you but is not the whole of who you are. Accept the hurt parts of yourself with loving compassion.

- Embrace what makes you unique.

- Identify what you value.

- Focus on your strengths.

- Set meaningful goals for the future.

- Mindfully release that which you cannot control.

- Intentionally choose to give grace to yourself day by day and moment by moment. It isn't easy being caught off guard by triggers, and of course you wish they would just go away. When you've worked hard at healing and are unexpectedly steamrolled by a trigger, it can be tempting to berate yourself for your feelings and reactions. Refuse and talk back to such self-criticism.

- Be purposeful with your self-talk, and permit only inner dialogue of reassurance, kindness, encouragement, and compassion.

- Allow yourself to be right where you are, and know that it's okay to be messy, imperfect, and in process. You are deserving of love (including self-love) just as you are.

LUPITA'S STORY

Lupita had thought of herself as "the throwaway kid" ever since she'd been kicked out. Once, her therapist had asked her if she loved that part of herself. Lupita had sobbed as she admitted that she only felt pity, disgust, and shame.

Many difficult sessions of processing her painful memories and feelings of being thrown away and abused had since transpired, and many tears shed. Lupita felt emotionally exhausted after some of those raw, honest therapy sessions but consistently soothed the activated emotions afterward by taking time in the privacy of her bedroom to follow along with a restorative yoga video. Without realizing it, Lupita was learning to love herself.

The shame melted away under the unwaveringly caring gaze of her therapist, and with it, the revulsion she felt toward herself for the things she had been made to do. The memories didn't become happy ones, but Lupita began to see her younger self with compassion and understanding. Eventually, Lupita realized that her answer had changed. "Remember when you asked me if I loved 'the throw-away kid'?" she asked her therapist one day. "Well, I finally do."

That part remained tucked inside her, cared for and quieted by her growing, wiser, compassionate self. It was no longer her identity. Instead, Lupita now saw herself as a strong, worthy, brave survivor.

I Have a Question . . .

I know I am more than what happened to me, but I'm afraid others won't

see it that way. When I imagine others knowing about what my coach

did to me, I worry they will think I'm bad or gross. So maybe I really

am tainted?

This is a tricky thing. You are absolutely right; you *are* so much more than what was done to you. I know that it doesn't always feel that way. But where you do have power is in how you speak to yourself about it, and how you present yourself to the world.

Continue to be mindful of your internal narrative, disallowing self-shaming talk. From that place of grounded truth, move through the world and in and out of interactions with the confidence that you are no less worthy than anyone else, nor are you bad or gross. While others may or may not have the mature, compassionate wisdom to see people for who they truly are, many others are capable of seeing the truth: that bad things often happen to good people. Hold your head high and refuse to evaluate yourself by the possible opinions of such immature people. Their hypothesized opinions would only reflect on them.

You get to choose, with thoughtful deliberation, with whom you can open up and share your story. If you notice that someone seems to engage with others in an open, nonjudgmental way, chances are that they will also see the truth about you: that you may be impacted, but are not tainted, by trauma.

Quiz: Where I Am Now

Take a moment to pause and assess where you are now and how far you have come. Celebrate and affirm yourself for how you have grown through the hard healing work you've engaged in thus far. Compassionately note where there remains room for continued growth.

True/Not Yet	I recognize that what happened was not my fault.
True/Not Yet	I release myself from blame.
True/Not Yet	I know the past does not define me.
True/Not Yet	I accept myself without condition—I don't have to do or accomplish anything.
True/Not Yet	I am lovable simply as I am.
True/Not Yet	I believe I am a good person.
True/Not Yet	I have one person or more whom I trust and with whom I feel safe.
True/Not Yet	I am meaningfully connected to others.
True/Not Yet	I have power and choices I can use to create a good life.
True/Not Yet	I have hope for the future.

Fill in the Blanks: Self-Concept Statements

Who are you, really? How would you describe your true self? What are the truths about you that you'd like the world to see? Complete the following sentence in as many ways as possible. This might be relational ("a playful babysitter"), metaphorical ("a lion"), descriptive ("passionate"), or anything that comes to you. You might reflect something like *I am strong . . . a fighter . . . brave . . . my own hero.* Stretch yourself to fill every blank and see what comes out. Then look over your answers and highlight those most meaningful to you.

I am _____. I am _____. I am _____.

I am _____. I am _____. I am _____.

I am _____. I am _____. I am _____.

I am _____. I am _____. I am _____.

I am _____. I am _____. I am _____.

PRACTICE: ENVISIONING MY FUTURE

One of the gifts of healing trauma while still in adolescence is that so much life is yet to be lived. As you make peace with the ugliness of the past, you can begin to shift toward facing the future. What dreams do you hold in your heart?

- *Close your eyes and begin to slow and deepen your breath. Hold in your mind one of the affirmations about your future that you developed in chapter 4, perhaps something like "I have limitless potential." Let the words settle in your heart.*
- *Now bring your attention to the precious dream you hold for your future. Allow yourself to imagine it. Picture where you are, who's around you, what you see. Notice what you feel. Just sit with it for a bit, letting the dream grow and take up space inside you.*
- *Know that you can make this dream a reality. Think of your personal strengths and how they will bring you toward this future. Hold it all together and set an intention for the next step. Place your hands over your heart or belly to seal this intention as a commitment to yourself. When you're ready, open your eyes as you take a closing deep breath.*

Finding Your Strengths

In focusing on the painful past and the ways that you struggle as a result, it can be easy to lose sight of your strengths. And yet those strengths that you lean on help you heal. You are so much more than your pain and struggles. Examining your strengths will help you realize your *agency*, or how much you do have control over and can do. It will also help you counter feelings of helplessness while providing a grounded boost to your self-esteem.

Strengths include positive personal traits and talents. Traits are internal characteristics, such as compassion, creativity, intelligence, and determination. Talents are skills and abilities such as musical aptitude, foreign language abilities, or athletic prowess. While strengths often grow from some innate element of your temperament and genes, both your traits and talents are fostered and developed through practice and intention.

UNIQUELY YOU

Hopefully, as you read the introduction of what strengths are, some ideas sprang to mind as to what some of yours might be. Such self-awareness is the first step toward identifying your strengths. If you're not sure what strengths you have or even if you have any, there are a few steps you can follow to explore what they might be.

First, know that everyone has strengths. They won't necessarily be the same as your sibling's or friend's but are uniquely your own. To identify them, start by considering what interests you and where your passions lie. This may give you a hint or direction to explore.

Second, open yourself to feedback from others. Where it may be tempting to listen to negative self-talk and can even feel like bragging to admit you are good at things, it is healthy to acknowledge the good in you, and others may provide insights you don't see. If you aren't already receiving positive feedback, courageously ask people who know you well to share what they see. They may reveal areas of strength you weren't previously aware of as well as areas wherein you can grow. These areas present opportunities to develop greater strengths; try not to view those aspects as criticisms or personal attacks.

You can also take a strengths assessment test to help identify areas that motivate, inspire, and energize you. You might ask a school counselor for such a resource or simply do an internet search for "free strengths assessment" and use a tool you find online.

Finally, know that strengths and growth areas are not static. As you gain a greater sense of freedom and healing from the past, you may find more energy available to devote to pursuits that excite you. This can be a good time to develop new skills as you seek out novel, healthy experiences.

HEALING STRATEGIES

Allowing yourself to recognize and take pride in your true strengths fortifies you and creates a foundation to become all that you can be. As you recognize your existing and emerging strengths, consider how you can employ them in ways that excite and energize you. These might be avenues for you to shine, or for you to give to your community in ways that support others and make the world a better place.

If you have areas of strength that feel simultaneously limited by associated trauma, try Brainspotting therapy and ask about the *expansion model*. This approach can not only help you work through the trauma and free you from the ways it has held you back but also provide performance enhancement to help you grow beyond your former peak.

Consider not only how you can use your strengths now, but how you might develop them, and how they might lead you toward a fulfilling career and life.

- If you are a natural leader, look for leadership opportunities.

- If you are a compassionate and understanding person, look for ways to provide care.

- If you are an intelligent problem solver, get involved in exploring solutions to a problem you care about.

Your strengths are part of you. You may have been injured, but you are not broken.

I Have a Question . . .

I used to be great at gymnastics, until the accident. At a competition I fell doing a back handspring on the beam and broke my ankle while everyone watched. While I was recovering, I thought of all the abuse I'd put up with from my coach just to reach that point and what a waste it all was. It took several months to recover physically, and I'm still working on healing emotionally. Gymnastics was my whole identity and the one thing I was good at. Now I'm torn. I miss doing it, but I'm also afraid. Should I go back?

It sounds like gymnastics has been very important to you. At the same time, I suspect that it is not your only strength. Although there is no clear right or wrong answer to the question of whether to return to your sport, I encourage you to take this pause to explore who you are in other ways and discover the range of your strengths.

Many personal strengths you developed through participation go beyond physical skill. To reach that point in your performance, you clearly developed characteristics of persistence, self-discipline, drive, and dedication. These traits will benefit you throughout life. What else does your experience reveal about you?

The decision of whether to return or retire from gymnastics is very personal, and one to take your time with. Listen to your gut instinct. As you were being abused by your former coach, certainly you cannot return to them, but you might find a new coach provides a fresh start. Consider therapy to work through the trauma of both the abuse and the accident. Whatever you decide to do, coming from a grounded self-knowledge, is the right choice for you.

List: Identifying My Strengths

Having spent some time in reading and reflection regarding potential strengths, it's time to get practical. What are some of your own strengths? Consider physical, mental, social, and emotional categories. List your ideas in the table that follows. If you don't know what to put, ask trusted adults or friends for input. Don't be modest!

TRAITS	TALENTS
1.	1.
2.	2.
3.	3.
4.	4.
5.	5.

Fill in the Blanks: Future Strengths

Who do you want to be? What strengths do you admire in others? What would you like to develop in yourself as an area of potential growth? In addition to the valuable strengths you've listed previously, consider the boundless potential for growth you have as an adolescent. Consider the following sentence prompts as you imagine a future in which you grow and become all that you value and admire.

In the future, I see myself as _____.

I am becoming _____and

_____. I would like to work

on developing _____

_____ in myself. One trait I

admire in _____

that I would like to emulate is the ability to _____

_____.

Because my goal is to _____,

I am working on _____.

I believe in myself and know I can grow in my capacity for _____

_____.

Table: Strengths in Action

Use this table to explore and reinforce your strengths. In the boxes that follow, list your top four strengths, describe a time when you used each, how it felt as you did so, and the outcome. It's okay—even good—to feel pride in these things.

MY STRENGTH	HOW I USED IT	HOW IT FELT	THE OUTCOME

Determining Your Values

Values are the ideas and principles that guide your attitudes, actions, and decisions and determine what is important to you. They are not stagnant but can change throughout your life span, influenced by experiences and new learning. Not surprisingly, then, trauma usually has a significant impact on your value system. Traumatic experiences expose you to human, societal, or environmental problems in sharp detail, inevitably causing you to grapple with issues that others might have the privilege to ignore. As you wrestle with these things, you form values around what's important in society and the world, what you value in interpersonal relationships, and what rights are important to protect.

This can be a positive outcome of surviving trauma and an aspect of post-traumatic growth. Consciously identifying your values is an important element of maturity and allows you to become a mindful, purpose-driven individual with the potential to make a meaningful imprint on the world. Rather than thoughtlessly reacting, as a values-driven person you are empowered to make decisions and behave in ways that bring you closer to the future you want to inhabit.

Values are personal and subjective. There are endless possibilities and no clear right or wrong answer as to what you ought to value. Determining your values is part of what makes you *you*.

PERSONAL VALUES

So how do you figure out what you value? Start by considering what's important to you. What gets you fired up or motivates you to action? Are there injustices that you can't let go? When have you felt most like your true self? Write these ideas down.

Think about people you admire. What is it that draws you to them? Is it a characteristic such as integrity, kindness, or a sense of humor? Perhaps you have shared values of a commitment to athletic or academic excellence. These traits, reflected in others, may offer more clues.

Think of the major events of your life. This will include your traumatic experience but also other pivotal moments. What did you take from these experiences that illuminates what's important?

Now, look over your notes from these questions and see if there are any common themes. Group them together and notice what feels most important.

You might consider what other important people in your life seem to value. While some of these ideas could make it onto your own list, it's fine if they don't.

Your values are your own, and it is perfectly okay if they differ from those of your friends, parents, or even religious leaders. It is so beneficial that our world is filled with people with varying passions. Because one person can only care about and work toward so much, if we all shared the same passions, some important values would inevitably get ignored. You have an important place and role in this world as exactly who you are and are becoming.

HEALING STRATEGIES

After drawing up a list of core values, spend some time refining your definitions of each.

Consider:

- What does each concept mean to you?

- What does it look like in action?

- In what way is this value reflected in your life?

Continually test and examine whether you are living authentically to your values by asking yourself honest questions, such as:

- "Do my actions lately reflect this value?"

- "Am I creating opportunities for myself to express or practice this value?"

- "Am I putting myself in positions that stretch me to further develop this value?"

As you plan or consider future decisions, hold them up against your core values to determine whether your choices are congruent. This can help bring clarity to decision-making processes.

The more you align your actions and behaviors with your core values, the more you live in the grounded confidence of *integrity*. This brings a sense of peace, happiness, and flow to your life. You can shed guilt, gain greater focus, and enjoy healthier relationships as you live authentically.

LASHANDRA'S STORY

Growing up, LaShandra was constantly punished for things she did not do. Now sixteen and living with her aunt, she'd become keenly attuned to matters of injustice. She'd come to highly value her newfound ability to use her voice to speak for herself and advocate for others. As she leaned into these values of justice and free speech, LaShandra became a leader in her school and community. She led a rally on campus to raise awareness about racial profiling and police brutality, raising her voice about injustices against others. Taking it a step further, she and a few friends traveled to their state capitol to speak about these issues and appeal for systemic change. Although nothing could justify the abuse she had suffered as a younger child, as she healed from her wounds LaShandra found strength and purpose in her strong value system.

I Have a Question . . .

When I reflect on what is important to me, words like loyalty, family, *and* connection *come to mind. But since my whole family except me died in the car crash, I don't have those things anymore. Should I pick something else for my values? Something I can control?*

First of all, I'm so sorry you lost what was most important to you. As far as choosing your values, I'd suggest that you don't so much *select* them as *realize* them. You value family, connection, and loyalty because these are fundamentally precious and important to you, and that is part of who you are.

Hold on to what is dear to you. As you keep these values in your heart, you nurture the ideal, and keep your heart soft and open to these things. In so doing, you make space for them to grow again in new ways. Nothing will ever replace the devastating loss of your family at a young age. And yet, I hope for you that these values find new and additional ways to take root in your life, through friendships, extended family, mentors, and perhaps even a future family of your own making. Keep your heart open to connection and embody the loyalty you value.

MEDITATION PRACTICE: VALUES REFLECTION

- Settle yourself into a comfortable position. Begin to deepen and lengthen your breaths.
- Allow your mind to drift to a time when you felt happy, content, and fully yourself. Let yourself see and feel that moment and just sit with it for a while. What words come to mind describing what made this moment so good? Perhaps you identify it with adventure, freedom, peace, challenge, togetherness, creativity, or something else. Hold that value word in your mind as you continue to breathe deeply, in and out, allowing your belly to rise and fall.
- Notice where your eyes gaze as you meditate on this value. You might stay with that gaze spot, or experiment with looking in different directions. Notice where you are looking when the sense of connection to the value feels most present in your body. Stay there for a while. Just observe and see what images, thoughts, and feelings come up.
- Allow your mind to drift gradually to the future, holding together the grounded happiness you began with in the first image, the value you've identified, and an image of your future self. Picture yourself living out that value in new and meaningful ways. Let your mind linger there as long as you like.
- When you are ready, you can return to the present, stretching your body to accommodate and settle the new visions you've developed, knowing that this value-rich future is yours to make.

Checklist: My Values

The following is a list of fifty ideals. This is not a comprehensive list, so feel free to add your own. As you consider what drives and excites you, check off the values that resonate. Select up to ten that matter most to you, and then highlight your top three.

- ☐ Adventure
- ☐ Balance
- ☐ Beauty
- ☐ Compassion
- ☐ Connection
- ☐ Cooperation
- ☐ Creativity
- ☐ Diversity
- ☐ Endurance
- ☐ Equality
- ☐ Exploration
- ☐ Faith
- ☐ Family
- ☐ Financial independence
- ☐ Fitness
- ☐ Flexibility

- ☐ Forgiveness
- ☐ Freedom
- ☐ Friendship
- ☐ Fun
- ☐ Generosity
- ☐ Grace
- ☐ Harmony
- ☐ Health
- ☐ Honesty
- ☐ Humanity
- ☐ Humor
- ☐ Independence
- ☐ Integrity
- ☐ Intuition
- ☐ Justice
- ☐ Kindness
- ☐ Learning

- ☐ Love
- ☐ Loyalty
- ☐ Obedience
- ☐ Openness
- ☐ Order
- ☐ Peace
- ☐ Power
- ☐ Prosperity
- ☐ Reciprocity
- ☐ Reliability
- ☐ Sacrifice
- ☐ Safety
- ☐ Security
- ☐ Spirituality
- ☐ Strength
- ☐ Trust
- ☐ Truth

Calendar: Values in My Day

List your top three values in the left column of the calendar that follows. For each day of the week, note ideas of how you can take actions that engage that value. Check back with the calendar throughout and at the end of the week to stay focused, readjust, and reorient to your values and goals.

VALUE	SUNDAY	MONDAY	TUESDAY

WEDNESDAY	THURSDAY	FRIDAY	SATURDAY

Setting Your Goals

As you move through the healing process, you become freer to look ahead with a sense of hope and determination. What sort of future would you like to build? What goals serve as critical markers along the path to this vision?

Setting goals empowers you to create the future you want by breaking down a broad vision into concrete, attainable milestones. It provides markers you can achieve and celebrate along the way. For example, if you have a vision of a future in which you work as a teacher, you might work backward by setting a goal of attending college. This requires an intermediary goal of graduating from high school, and preliminary goals of doing well in and passing classes.

You are not caught by and stuck in the past that once may have felt so controlling, consuming, and hopeless. Setting concrete, specific, and realistic goals is a tangible reminder that you are an overcomer, you are free, and you can be the hero of your own story.

GETTING SMART

So how do you create practical and useful goals to propel you toward the future you want to create? A solid goal is SMART: *specific, measurable, attainable, relevant*, and *timebound*.

A *specific* goal narrows down your vision to something concrete. This helps you clarify how and where to begin. The big question to ask in defining this is "What do I want to do?" For example, you might say, "I want to graduate from high school with honors," or "I want to make more friends."

Your goal becomes *measurable* when you determine how to quantify your progress. Using our examples, you can measure your progress toward graduating with honors by identifying the grades required and the percentages needed for those grades. The goal of making more friends can become measurable by quantifying the number of friends you desire to make.

A good goal is *attainable*. Setting a goal to become the best NBA player in the world is nearly impossible, and thus a poor motivator. A goal of increasing your rate of successful shots from 2/3 to 9/10 is a goal that you could work toward while tracking your progress.

Be sure to set goals that are *relevant* to your values and life vision. As with our example about becoming a teacher, a goal of attending college, and therefore of graduating from high school, is directly relevant to the overall direction. This might be supported by a value of wanting to nurture children or help others succeed. A goal disconnected from a broader vision or set of internalized values is one that you are likely to abandon.

Finally, create *timebound* goals. Giving yourself parameters within which to meet your goals will keep you on track. I spent many years vaguely planning to write books one day, but until I had concrete deadlines, I didn't get much writing done. Similarly, if your goal is to make two new friends, you might specify plans to invite two classmates to hang out by the end of fall semester.

HEALING STRATEGIES

As you create your goals and consider the short-, medium-, and long-term milestones to achieve, check in with yourself. Remain grounded in the truth that your intrinsic worth is separate from your goals. Believe that you have what it takes and can accomplish what you set out to do, and that you do deserve to achieve happiness and satisfaction and to have good things. Don't let self-doubt and negative self-talk sabotage you. Know that you are enough already, just as you are, and you do not need to achieve anything to prove your worth. Then, grounded in these essential truths, take courage and push forward to realize your dreams!

Here are a few strategies to help you achieve your goals:

Find a mentor. If you lack clarity on how to reach your goal, someone who has relevant experience can provide invaluable encouragement along the way.

- Reach out to people who are knowledgeable about the thing you want to do, who have done it, or are doing it themselves.

- Introduce yourself, then boldly and respectfully ask for guidance.

Envision your big-picture goal and take notes.

- Identify the milestones needed to accomplish your goal, and break those down further into details.

- Organize these pieces into a progressive plan of action.

- Cross off each step as you do it to record your progress and successes along the way.

Remain mindfully focused on the steps right in front of you so that you don't become overwhelmed. Piece by piece, day by day, you *will* realize your goal.

List: Goals

In the space that follows, list some of your personal goals for each category.

Personal/Relational:

_____.

_____.

_____.

_____.

Academic/Career:

_____.

_____.

_____.

_____.

Hobbies/Extracurricular:

_____.

_____.

_____.

_____.

Emotional/Mental Health:

_____.

_____.

_____.

_____.

Physical Health:

_____.

_____.

_____.

_____.

Spiritual Well-Being:

_____.

_____.

_____.

_____.

Table: Setting SMART Goals

Use the table that follows to clarify and make concrete one or two personal goals. If you only have one goal you are aspiring to at this time, feel free to leave the second column blank to return to when it is useful to you.

	GOAL 1	GOAL 2
Specific: *(What is my goal? Who is involved? Where will it happen?)*		
Measurable: *(How will I know I am making progress toward this goal?)*		
Attainable: *(Is this something I can realistically do? What resources do I have or can I gather?)*		
Relevant: *(How is this connected to my big picture? Why am I doing this?)*		
Timebound: *(What is my anticipated time line for beginning and for completion?)*		

Table: My Short-, Mid-, and Long-Term Goals

Bringing the pieces together, identify two personal goals. Note the core personal values that drive you toward this vision, clarify the overarching goal and what it will look like when you've achieved it, and note the medium- and short-range goals along the envisioned path. Finally, tie it all together by reflecting on your personal strengths upon which you can draw to support and sustain progress toward these worthy goals.

	GOAL 1	GOAL 2
Driving value:		
Long-term goal:		
Medium-range milestones:		
Short-term stepping-stones:		
Supporting strengths:		

I am free.

~~~~~~

I have hope.

~~~~~~

My future is bright.

Key Takeaways

- Affirming that what happened was not your fault and is not what defines you can provide freedom to accept yourself as you are.

- The past will have impacted and shaped you somewhat, but it is not *who you are*.

- You have many strengths, including both traits and talents, that make you unique.

- Identifying your values can give you a sense of direction and purpose.

- Drawing from these values and building on your strengths, you can set goals that will empower you to create the future you dream of and desire.

- You are worthy and deserving of good things. Allow yourself acceptance, self-love, and room to dream.

RESOURCES

Apps

Bearable: *free or paid versions; track moods, meds, exercise, sleep, food*

Breathing: *free; guides you in simple, calming breath work*

Calm: *annual fee; meditation and anxiety management app*

Calm Harm: *free; for teens struggling with self-harm*

Daily Affirmation: *free; provides a new positive affirmation every day*

Headspace: *monthly or annual fee; meditation app includes sleep meditations*

Insight Timer: *free; guided meditations*

PTSD Coach: *free; helps manage PTSD with education, resources, and tools*

Recovery Road: *free app to help overcome eating disorders*

Shine: *annual fee; mental health support and online community for BIPOC*

Books

Carter, Lee. *It Happened to Me: A Teen's Guide to Overcoming Sexual Abuse.* New Harbinger, 2002.

Libin, Nicole. *5-Minute Mindfulness Meditations for Teens.* Rockridge Press, 2019.

Lohman, Raychelle Cassad. *The Sexual Trauma Workbook for Teen Girls: A Guide to Recovery from Sexual Assault and Abuse.* Instant Help, 2016.

MacCutcheon, Megan. *The Ultimate Self-Esteem Workbook for Teens: Overcome Insecurity, Defeat Your Inner Critic, and Live Confidently.* Althea Press, 2019.

Nathan, Brenda. *The One-Minute Gratitude Journal for Teens: Simple Journal to Increase Gratitude and Happiness.* BrBB, 2020.

Nelson, Tammy. *What's Eating You? A Workbook for Teens with Anorexia, Bulimia, and Other Eating Disorders*. Instant Help, 2008.

Peter, Val J., and Dowd, Tom. *Boundaries: A Guide for Teens*. Boys Town Press, 2020.

Vinall, Deborah. *Gaslighting: A Step-by-Step Recovery Guide to Heal from Emotional Abuse and Build Healthy Relationships*. Rockridge Press, 2021.

Crisis Help Lines

Childhelp: 800-4-A-CHILD (422-4453)
24/7 assistance and information on child abuse

Love Is Respect: 800-331-9474 or text 22522
24/7 dating violence hotline

National Human Trafficking Hotline: 888-373-7888 or text 233733
24/7 help for victims and survivors of human trafficking

National Runaway Safeline: 800-RUNAWAY (786-2929)
24/7 hotline for youth on the run or considering running away

National Sexual Assault Hotline: 800-656-4673
24/7 help for victims of sexual assault, rape, or incest

National Suicide Prevention Lifeline: 800-273-TALK (8255)
24/7 support and assistance for people feeling depressed or suicidal

Substance Abuse and Mental Health Services Administration helpline:
    800-662-HELP (4357)
*24/7 treatment referral and information for those with substance use and mental
    health problems*

Trevor Project: 866-488-3000
24/7 crisis and suicide prevention hotline for LGBTQ youth

Trans Lifeline: 877-565-8860 (USA); 877-330-6366 (Canada)
Trans peer support run by and for trans people. Hours may vary.

Websites

Brainspotting Directory Brainspotting.com/directory
    Searchable directory to find a certified Brainspotting therapist near you

EMDRIA Find a Therapist EMDRIA.org/find-an-emdr-therapist
    *Searchable directory to find a certified EMDR (Eye Movement Desensitization
    and Reprocessing) therapist near you*

NEDA NationalEatingDisorders.org/help-support/contact-helpline
    Help for eating disorders

NIDA Teens.DrugAbuse.gov
    National Institute on Drug Use for Teens

RAINN RAINN.org
    Anti-sexual violence organization

Stop Bullying StopBullying.gov
    *Tips on recognizing and responding safely to in-person bullying and
    cyber-bullying*

Teen's Health KidsHealth.org/en/teens/about.html
    Doctor-reviewed advice on physical, behavioral, and emotional health for teens

Trevor Project TheTrevorProject.org
    Resources, information, and support for LGBTQ youth

REFERENCES

"2006 Sleep in America Poll: Summary of Findings." National Sleep Foundation: Accessed September 3, 2021. TheNSF.org/wp-content/uploads/2021/03/2006 -SIA-summary_of_findings.pdf.

Creswell, J. David, et al. "Self-Affirmation Improves Problem-Solving Under Stress." *PLOS ONE* 8, no. 5 (May 1, 2013). DOI.org/10.1371/journal.pone.0062593.

Epton, T., P. R. Harris, R. Kane, G. M. van Koningsbruggen, and P. Sheeran. "The Impact of Self-Affirmation on Health-Behavior Change: A Meta-Analysis." *Health Psychology* 34, no. 3 (2015): 187–196.

Gordon, Harold W. "Differential Effects of Addictive Drugs on Sleep and Sleep Stages." *Journal of Addiction Research (OPAST Group)* 3, no. 2 (2019). DOI.org/10.33140/JAR.03.02.01.

Hamby, S., D. Finkelhor, H. Turner, and R. Ormrod. "The Overlap of Witness-ing Partner Violence with Child Maltreatment and Other Victimizations in a Nationally Representative Survey of Youth." *Child Abuse & Neglect* 34, no. 10 (2010): 734–741. DOI.org/10.1016/j.chiabu.2010.03.001 (as cited by Courtois, Christine, and Julian Ford. *Treatment of Complex Trauma: A Sequenced, Relationship-Based Approach*. Guilford Press, 2013).

Johnshoy-Currie, Connie. The 6 F's of Trauma Response, Dissociative Disruptions, and the Development of Dissociative Identity Disorder (DID). Personal commu-nication, 2020.

Roades, A. "Claiming Peaceful Embodiment Through Yoga in the Aftermath of Trauma." *Contemporary Therapies in Clinical Practice* 21 (2015): 247–256. ResearchGate.net/publication/283193438_Claiming_Peaceful_Embodiment _Through_Yoga_in_the_Aftermath_of_Trauma.

Rosen, Michael, and Helen Oxenbury. *We're Going on a Bear Hunt*. 1989. Walker Books.

Shifeng, Li, Wu Yiling, Zhang Fumin, Xu Qiongying, and Zhou Aibao. "Self-Affirmation Buffering by the General Public Reduces Anxiety Levels During the COVID-19 Epidemic." *Acta Psychologica Sinica* 52, no. 7 (2020): 886-894. journal.Psych.AC.cn/acps/EN/10.3724/SP.J.1041.2020.00886.

West, J., B. Liang, and J. Spinazzola, J. "Trauma Sensitive Yoga as a Complementary Treatment for Posttraumatic Stress Disorder: A Qualitative Descriptive Analysis." *International Journal of Stress Management* 24, no. 2 (2017): 173-195. DOI.org/10.1037/str0000040.

Yücel, Murat, et al. "Regional Brain Abnormalities Associated with Long-Term Heavy Cannabis Use." *Archives of General Psychiatry* 65, no. 6 (2008): 694-701. DOI.org/10.1001/archpsyc.65.6.694.

INDEX

Acknowledgments

Although writing may be a solitary process, no work is created in isolation. The efforts and creativity of the editorial and design teams at Callisto have shaped this work to be the beautiful volume you hold in your hands today. This book would not be possible without the endless support and encouragement of my wonderful husband, Shane, who has always believed in me, cheered me on, and worked alongside me late into the night. Thank you to my son, Luke, for encouraging me and for being your sweet self, and to my dear friends for your support—you know who you are, and I hope you know how much you mean to me. Dr. Chris D'Arcy, thank you for generously sitting with me and reviewing my neuroscience references. Thank you to my many mentors, teachers, and colleagues who have guided me along the way in becoming the therapist I am today; your impact is reflected in these pages as well as in my heart.

About the Author

Deborah Vinall, PsyD, LMFT, is a certified EMDR and Brainspotting practitioner, and a trained Trauma Sensitive Yoga (TC-TSY) instructor. She specializes in helping individuals heal from traumatic life experiences and painful relationship dynamics through her private practice, Tamar Counseling Services. Deborah is also the author of *Gaslighting: A Step-by-Step Recovery Guide to Heal from Emotional Abuse and Build Healthy Relationships*. She was awarded the Sandra Wilson Memorial Grant from the EMDR Research Foundation for her research on the impacts and treatment response of survivors of mass shootings across the United States. A native of Kelowna, Canada, Deborah presently makes her home in Southern California with her husband, teenage son, and two semi-feral cats. Find her online at DrDeborahVinall.com.